Shrimp Tales

Port Isabel and Brownsville Shrimping History

RUDY H. GARCIA
PAT MCGRATH AVERY

Library of Congress Control Number: 2019956736

ISBN: 978-1-943267-73-6

Cover Art: Risa E. Garcia

Edited and Designed by Joyce Faulkner

Printed in the United States.

Red Engine Press

Do You Know a Shrimper?

Have you ever looked into the eyes of a weathered old shrimper?
Have you ever touched his monstrous, calloused hands?
Have you ever noticed his tired shoulders once broad?
His crab claw like powerful arms, tattooed and scarred.

Have you noticed that his worn sea face is unlike yours and mine?
Have you ever wondered why he continually ventures back
out to sea?
Have you ever prayed that he returns from there safe and sound?
Have you ever been there on the mooring docks, to welcome
him home?

On Board a Shrimp Boat

Have you ever been aboard a shrimping boat?
With the Captain and his mates.
Have you ever held a deep-sea trawling net
And wondered how the shrimp get in?
Or have you ever pulled a heavy sea-soaked cabo rope
That carves and measures the fathoms deep.

Have you ever paced a shrimp boat's slippery deck?
Or stood by anchor's prow,
Have you ever had an angry wave
Slap you mercilessly across the face?
Have you ever climbed the towering mainmast?
During bitter cold winters or tropic tempest storms.

Have you ever fallen overboard, way far, too far from shore?
Never seen or heard of again, never to be held again,

Never to be hugged again, never, never more.

Have you ever, ever, been the one, the one with endless love?

The patient father, rosary-praying mother – who lost a son at sea.

Have you ever been the loving wife to kiss his lips no more?

Have you ever been the admiring child who lost a Dad at sea?

Have you ever known a shrimping man who lost his life at sea?

Many Days Out at Sea

Have you ever been too long, too many days away at sea?

And missed your newborn baby's birth,

His very first gay filled mirth,

Or when he climbed his first tall tree?

Were you around even to see?

And hear him say, 'look dad, dad look at me!'

Have you even been too far out at sea?

Away from children's glee,

Too far to hear that blissful sound,

Unable to stroke their shiny crown,

Too far to comfort the weeping child,

And wipe away a pouting frown

Or tuck away your babe's goodnight,

Then morrow keep them in your constant sight.

Have you ever toiled too long at sea?

Have you ever spent too many days and nights of yesterday?

Trawling for shrimp, then washing riggings packed with
oceans' bottom clay,

Mending nets, constantly coiling ropes, charting the course for the
next sailing day,

Thirty-forty-fifty-sixty days, sailed out in March, docking back
sometime in May.

Have you ever scrubbed and scrubbed and rubbed, then washed,
shampooed your briny body?
From the embedded—penetrated under your skin—smell
of the salty sea?
Of slimy netted shrimp gunk, of chocking black bellowing
exhaust diesel fumes,
Or rusted iron from your hands, of slippery by-catch, staining
your white rubber deck boots.
Have you ever smelled a shrimper man who toiled too long at sea?

Have you ever been so long at sea?
To never hear your son's first a, b, c,
Your daughter's first count of 1, 2, 3,
Not there to see them off for their first day of school
Or tell them both about the guiding golden rule
Or how the sea is composed of countless globules
upon tiny globules.

Have you ever stayed that long at sea?

Rudy H. Garcia

First published in *Two Eagles*

CONTENTS

1

INTRODUCTION

Texas (photo taken at Zimco Marine)

Best shrimp in the world!
Once you've tasted wild-caught Gulf of Mexico shrimp, you
never want any other.

THESE TYPICAL COMMENTS BY Port Isabel and
South Padre Island, Texas, visitors are music to the
ears of shrimpers, restaurants, and shrimp markets.
Unquenchable appetites keep the demand for quality

shrimp strong. The appetite and demand for wild-caught Gulf of Mexico shrimp is so high that local shrimpers navigate and trawl their nets offshore along the bottom of the Gulf from the mouth of the Rio Grande River, up and down the entire Texas coast, Louisiana coast east and west, Mississippi, Alabama, Florida's northwest coast, its west coast and all the way south to Key West.

The size, quality, and freshness of Gulf of Mexico shrimp raise the bar for outstanding seafood. American consumers have other sources of shrimp besides the "preferred for its great taste" wild-caught Gulf shrimp. Some come from the southeastern part of the United States, some from the western and northwestern part of the country—and some from other countries that have a shrimping industry. However, the majority of shrimp are imported into the United States from shrimp farming countries. These sell for a cheaper price, enticing many restaurant chains and grocery stores to buy and resell them to their customers.

These farm-raised shrimp do not compare well, nor measure up to the taste, nutritional value, and benefits of our Gulf of Mexico shrimp. Wild-caught Gulf shrimp are harvested from their natural habitat. They grow and develop as Mother Nature intended, under flowing-ocean currents, free of any human-fed chemicals in dirty, stagnant man-made ponds.

Listen to and speak with local generational residents about their love for wild-caught Gulf shrimp long enough and you'll learn about the slight yet distinct taste differences and body texture between white, brown, and pink shrimp. Although some swear by the difference, it is subtle. All three come from the nurturing bottom of the Gulf of Mexico. However, the firmness of the body and meat may vary. Experienced shrimpers are of the opinion that the brown shrimp is the firmest of the three.

As far as the best tasting is concerned, you have to be an experienced consumer with trained, discriminating-taste buds to tell the difference in a blind test. It's a matter of preference. Brown shrimp contain more iodine giving them a stronger flavor. The white shrimp are sweeter. The pink, which is found around the Florida Keys, south Florida, and the Bay of Campeche, Mexico, is milder and sweeter-tasting than the other two. The most commonly-consumed, wild-caught shrimp today is the brown, because it is plentiful and preferred by the marketplace. During the upstart years of the shrimping boom, production and buyers in the Midwest, Chicago, and New York preferred the brown. Shrimpers found they were easier to sell. Brown shrimp are found offshore in deep water while the white and pink are closer to shore, a short distance from the beach.

It is common for residents and visitors to Port Isabel and South Padre Island to see shrimp boats venturing out beyond the safe harbor of the Brazos de Santiago Pass. Typical sea excursions are lengthy and far away as the shrimpers search for the much-desired wild-caught Gulf shrimp.

Most of us have had the pleasure of watching the movie, *Forrest Gump*. In several scenes his best army friend, Bubba, "who knew everything there is to know about shrimping" educates and enlightens Forest about the many different ways of preparing and cooking shrimp, giving us an understanding and appreciation as to why the demand for wild-caught Gulf shrimp is so high.

BLUE AND GOLD—THE COLORS OF PORT ISABEL

The Laguna Madre and the Gulf of Mexico have many moods and many shades of blue. There are days the bay changes from turquoise to a deep blue and other days where the blue turns gray. On windy days when the sand rolls, there will still be patches of blue amid the sandy bay water.

Climb atop the lighthouse on a sunny day and the causeway cuts a stripe across the blue water, presenting a delightful view. Whether you follow the island coast to the north or to the south, it is the blue of the water that enchants you.

Stroll around town and you're sure to see someone in a blue Port Isabel High School Tarpon shirt.

Gold came to Port Isabel in the form of shrimp boats—and hard-working men and women. While the town prospered or languished in different eras, one thing remained constant. It was a paradise for fishing and recreation. In the early 1900s, few ways to make a living existed. The wealthy came to play. The residents catered to their needs—and the burgeoning tourist industry was born.

World War II changed the average American's life in many ways. Port Isabel fishermen benefited from the surplus supply of diesel engines at the war's end. More powerful and efficient than the gas engines of the 1930s and before, the diesel enabled larger and faster boats.

Change came in the form of shrimpers from North Carolina and Louisiana seeking new opportunities. With their larger boats with diesel engines, they came to take advantage of Port Isabel's easy access to Mexican waters. The small town soon began to flourish. There were more shrimp than the shrimpers could imagine. For them, these blue waters turned to gold.

The shrimp were plentiful, huge, and delicious. Local fishermen, who had shrimped in the bay and along the Gulf shore for generations, joined the newcomers—building bigger boats and fishing the deeper waters of the Gulf of Mexico.

America's taste for shrimp began to grow, slowly at first. Once developed, the country's voracious appetite turned shrimping into a gold mine.

During the 1940s–1970s, boats carried ice. Headed shrimp could be safely stored about ten days. Freezers changed the industry by allowing boats to stay out at sea for longer periods.

For approximately thirty years, shrimpers prospered. Opportunities for work grew and new related businesses opened. Most people made a living; some became millionaires. Young residents learned the industry at an early age. Girls helped in the fish houses while boys worked on the boats. Almost every business in town related to shrimping—boat builders, net makers, diesel repair shops, grocery stores, ice houses, and other suppliers.

When shrimp boats returned, the town siren sounded and horns honked. The town went to work. All able-bodied residents made their way to the fish houses where they headed the shrimp and packed them for shipping.

SAFETY AND COMPATIBILITY

Shrimping excursions keep the boats and crew (three to four crew members, captain, rig-man, and one to two headers) out at sea an average of forty-five to sixty days. That is a long time to live and work together. Maintaining friendly attitudes towards one another in the cramped living space of a seventy-to-eighty-foot-long marine fishing vessel is not easy. It takes a special captain to keep order and civility.

Working on a shrimp boat is hazardous. There are too many things that can go wrong. Safety is the most important part of the captain's job. He is responsible for everything that happens on board his boat, good or bad. Therefore, from the time they cast off until they return to port, he works to instill safety-awareness in his crew—so that everyone returns alive and injury free to their wives, children, and parents.

Winches, cables, ropes and pulleys, nets, chains, anchors, towering main masts, outstretched arms of the outriggers and trawling doors[1]—all of these parts are integral to bringing up shrimp from the bottom of the ocean for heading,[2] sorting, washing, cleaning, packing, freezing, and storage.

An organized order for all of this equipment exists. Everything has its place, use, and purpose. But the fact remains that these men work in rough seas, frigid gales, and freak storms. No matter how sure the crew thinks they tied down all of these hazards, Mother Nature has her own more powerful way of ripping everything loose.

FIRST NIGHTS

The first few nights during the beginning of every new shrimping season in Texas, which starts around the middle of July, shrimp boat captains fish close to port, not far offshore. When opening day arrives all of the

1   Big wooden and steel door-like equipment needed to keep open the mouth of the nets as they drag along the Gulf bottom
2   Squeezing heads off shrimp

boats are fully rigged, prepared, and fueled to capacity. The captain and boat owners inspect every possible operational detail. Nothing is left to chance. A lot of money has been invested. The first few days determine whether the upcoming shrimp season will be profitable, break-even, or a loss. Almost all boat owners take out bank loans to finance the purchase of fuel, nets, riggings, ice, and money advancements to the captain and crew. They use their boats as collateral to secure the bank note.

Before even leaving the mooring docks, boat owners are already thousands of dollars in debt. They gamble that Mother Nature will be generous to them. They gamble that the boat will survive the first few days without any mechanical break downs, bad weather that may not allow them to shrimp, or injury to crew members. It's a nail-biting time of year. As soon as the boats clear the jetties and reach their fishing spots, they drop their nets. Owners wait by their side band radio, listening to the captains talking to one another as they report their try nets counts.[3]

During the first few fishing nights, captains rarely radio the boat owners to report their catch status. Owners, out of respect to the captains do not contact them, asking how they are doing. They patiently wait and listen to the radio. They learn how things are going by listening to the captains talk back and forth. The captains after all are experienced fisherman and know how to adjust to the try net counts. Most have been shrimping since they were young men in their teens. Through their many years at sea they accumulated and

---

3   Try nets are small nets that captains use to gauge whether or not the spot on the Gulf floor they chose for their first trawl has any shrimp.

charted numerous fishing grounds As captains, they have much on their minds. The owners took a gamble on them and handed over their prides and livelihoods. However, they realize the anticipated payout they took on the new shrimping season is not on the captain's competency, but the fear that the boat's rigging, engine, and other essential equipment does not break down, forcing the boat's return to the dock for repairs. They have worked together for many years or know of their productive reputation. All shrimp boat owners know each other. The same goes for captains and rig men, the two ranking members of each crew.

Word of mouth reputation and recommendations regarding the abilities and effectiveness of both captains and rig men travel fast in the shrimping community. A boat owner is not about to hand over the operation of his boat, worth tens of thousands of dollars, to a careless captain. A good rig man will not sign on to rig with a character-flawed captain. Both the boat owners and the rig men are into the new shrimp season for the same reason—to make money. Lots of money. Fishing with and handing over their boats to a captain with a bad fishing record is a risk neither rig men nor boat owners are willing to take.

There are, and will always be, mechanical malfunctions on board shrimp boats. A good captain will assess the problem and with the help of his crew, try to fix the mechanical failure himself. Correcting the problem out at sea enables the boat to continue catching shrimp and making money. If the mechanical breakdown forces the captain to return to the dock for repairs, it creates loss of both time and money. Mechanical repairs to shrimp boats are expensive. The owner and boat are already operating with a significant debt. Add on costly repairs and the anticipated profit dwindles. A healthy shrimp boat will work hard, catch enough shrimp to pay back the borrowed money, pay the crew—and have enough left over to pay for incidental minor repairs such as ripped or torn nets that need mending, busted ropes, electrical malfunctions, and the list goes on.

One of the captain's responsibilities is to keep a list of everything that breaks down or needs to be replaced. Soon after the captain docks the boat port side, he will meet with the boat owner, give a quick safety report on the crew, and inform the owner how many boxes of shrimp he caught.[4]

The total number of boxes always ranks first in the owner's mind. The more boxes brought into port for sale, the bigger the profits. The size of the shrimp ranks second. The quality and condition of the shrimp is squeezed in between first and second. If the shrimp is not iced down and taken care of properly, it will not keep well. Lowering prettiness and quality results in less profit.

Everyone who works in the shrimp business—from crew members and boat owners to dockside workers—absolutely loves scooping up a handful of shrimp to admire and show off to others. Sometimes when a captain is proud of his catch, he will take a great big bite of one of them and swallow it raw!

The captain and owner go over the details of the expedition, including successes, failures, and other

---

4   Shrimp catches are measured in terms of boxes. Each box represents one hundred pounds of shrimp. No matter the size of the shrimp, small, medium or large, each box will always represent one hundred pounds. The larger the shrimp, the higher the price.

important issues. The captain produces a list of gear and supplies needing either repair or replacement. He then returns to the boat to give the crew and dock workers instructions for unloading the catch.

Although the captain and crew may not have thousands of dollars invested in the boat and supplies, they have a vested interest in the success of the first few nights of fishing. The boat crew gets a thirty-five-to-forty percent return on the final sale of their catch. Everyone is thinking money twenty-four/seven.

Fatigue does not come into play during the first few nights. There is no mind set for it. Experienced crew members know what awaits them as far as work is concerned. First timers have absolutely no idea of the torturous, mind boggling work they will experience as they sail beyond the pristine white sand dunes of Isla Blanca Beach.

THE FIRST-TIMERS' LAMENT

Once the boat clears the jetties and begins to glide up the front face of swelling waves, first-timers may ask themselves, "What the hell am I doing here?" They pass wave after wave tumbling toward the beaches of South Padre Island. As seafaring gulls and pelicans soar and hover above the approaching swells in search of their next helping of fish, shrimp, or crab, the first-timer begins to feel nauseous. As seasickness fells him, he soon wonders, "What did I get myself into?"

When the first catch is dumped on the deck, newbies see bewildered creatures of all shapes and sizes, flapping and scurrying in all directions, searching for a way to return back to their underwater world.

"Why am I sitting on this tiny bench, three inches off a wet slippery deck with a three-foot-high mound of netted sea life? I thought I was here to catch shrimp."

Every first-timer is warned by the captain, rig man, and other experienced shrimpers that the job is not an easy one. It is demanding. Everyone is expected to pull his own weight. Once he signs on for a trip there is no turning back. Once those boat ropes are turned loose from the mooring docks and the captain pushes the throttle forward, cranking up the powerful diesel engine, that's it.

The huge engines produce bellowing, suffocating burnt diesel fumes. Shrimpers can't help but breathe in the black diesel exhaust. The first-timer soon experiences a sore and aching back, tired arms and legs, and most of all, bruised, cut and swollen hands from heading thousands upon thousands of shrimp. Add to that the pulling, coiling and uncoiling of rough, heavy, salt water-soaked ropes that burn deep into his blistering hands. It will do no good to complain. No one cares. The shrimp catch is the only thing that matters. More shrimp to catch. More shrimp to head. The more shrimp you head, the more money in your pockets.

Lack of sleep is not an issue nor is it a problem. It's part of the job. It's expected. Cup after cup of coffee suffices. Throw in a few ice-cold soda pops and keep working.

Chain smoking packs of duty-free cigarettes keeps nicotine flowing into the blood stream. Together, the caffeine and nicotine allows the body to continue working until the last bobbing marketable shrimp is headed and stowed on its bed of ice.

For the most part the endless chain of cigarette smoke is not fully inhaled. They are lit, placed between chapped, cracked lips, and left to dangle.

Mingled in with all the coffee, soda, and cigarettes, crew members keep each other pumped up with jokes, songs, and chants of "money, money, money." There is no time for exhaustion or pain during the critical first few nights of fishing.

Food helps. They gobble down ham and cheese sandwiches between trawls throughout the long exhausting nights. A hearty mid-morning breakfast consists of a couple dozen eggs, two to three pounds of fried bacon, biscuits, bread or flour tortillas, more coffee, and a gallon of ice-cold milk.

Debilitating seasickness can last for hours or days. In either case, the captain expects his crew to keep working.

The novice constantly hears the captain and rig man barking orders and instructions. "It's time to set and let the nets down! Stand here! Move there! Grab that rope! Be quick about it!" Command after command. All the while, he moves here, he moves there. He grabs this and he grabs that. He does everything they tell him while he tries to ignore the sickness in his stomach.

Staggering to and fro, he tries as hard as he can to maintain his balance on top of the stern deck, which keeps moving up—and dropping back down. Then without warning, he finds himself standing firm on an even-planed deck. That respite lasts an instant before he plunges weightless, straight down eight feet or so landing between the void of the swelling waves. The boat vibrates and creaks. Clanking sounds come from its bowels. He looks around to see any sign or word from the captain that the boat is about to shatter and break apart.

The captain's order to abandon ship doesn't come. He merely continues getting ready to drop his nets into the water for fishing. The rig man too goes on about his job, standing at the controls of the powerful winch. His calloused hands grip the steel levers that control the spooled sets of cables—one to his left and the other to his immediate right. His right foot on the large brake located in front of him, he cautiously pulls out the lever releasing the cable and bridles tattered to the nets and fishing doors. The nets descend into the water. They are followed by the two doors—one on each side of the net. They instantly take water. The forward drive of the boat causes them to spread open as wide as the attached bridles allow. With his foot on the pedal, the rig man brakes the descent of his nets, making sure they drop evenly on either side of the boat all the way to the bottom of the Gulf—ready to swallow everything in their path.

The captain is at the helm steering his charted course. The nets are in the water. The creaking boat is riding up and down, rolling left and right with the endless rise and eddying motion of the sea. As the boat pushes forward, the nets below drag the pitch-black floor of the Gulf of Mexico.

The rig man, satisfied that the nets are where they're supposed to be, turns to his header, giving him a reassuring expression that all is well. He knows and understands that the first-timer is nervous and oblivious to what is happening. He will be the teacher, his mentor, his safety line and perhaps maybe even a friend. But he will not be kind and gentle towards him. Gentleness has no place on board a shrimp boat.

These are rugged men. They live a tough, hard life. Shrimpers seem to adopt the same characteristics as the sea—tranquil at times, rough at others, but mostly rough. Their safety and survival requires that they be strong and rugged. They have to adapt to working with frequent pain and injury. There are no medical doctors or clinics out at sea. The only source of medical treatment for minor issues is each other—and a first-aid kit, aspirin, bandages, and some anti-bacterial ointment.

The rig man demands that his protégé be a quick and fast learner. The captain will not assume much, if any, of the teaching. That is not his responsibility. He assigns this role to his rig man. The rig man and the header will work side by side throughout the duration of the trip. The only time the rig man and the header are not within immediate proximity to each other is after the rig man reports to the captain that the nets are in the water and the stern deck is ready and prepped for the first "pick-up."[5]

Although the captain does not have time to teach, the first-timer learns plenty from him. By observing the captain's every decision and command, the newbie learns the captain's needs and desires. He understands that the captain's word is total and absolute law and his every command must be obeyed without question.

5   Pick-up refers to function of bringing up the nets from their trawl at the bottom of the Gulf to empty their contents on deck for sorting and heading of shrimp

THE RIG MAN, THE TRY-NET AND HIS FIRST WATCH

After reporting to the captain that the nets are in the water and the stern deck is prepped and ready for work, the captain tells the rig man the first course for fishing he has set—what trawling speed to maintain, how many minutes to travel in which direction before turning the boat back in the opposite direction. The captain also tells the rig man at what time intervals to check the try net to get a shrimp count. After these instructions are given, the captain passes the wheel and first watch to the rig man and retires to his bunk for a couple hours before picking up the first drag of the night. The try-net is a much smaller net than the bigger forty-foot-long trawling nets on either side of the boat. It is located at the rear of the shrimp boat. It does its job the same way as the larger nets except it stays in the water less time.

It's called a try-net because that is its purpose. The net is dropped to the bottom where it is dragged from fifteen to thirty minutes. It is then brought back up on deck, emptied, and the shrimp are counted. The size of the shrimp is also noted.

During the first watch when the rig man is at the wheel, he becomes the skipper. He has control of the boat and is responsible for everyone's safety. Before leaving the boat steering wheel unattended, to go back deck to check the try-net, he must make sure it's safe for him to do so. He has to peer deep into the dark night, looking for any flicker of lights in front, behind or to the sides of him. If he does see a light or lights on other marine vessels, he has to determine in which direction they are traveling—if they are headed his way or moving away from him. If they are coming toward him, does he have enough time to get out of their way to avoid a collision at sea? He has to distinguish if the lights he sees are red or green—red meaning port side, green starboard. These approaching lights indicate whether the other boat will pass to the right or left of him. A bright white light tells him that he is coming up on the rear of a boat. He also has the side-band radio.[6]

At this point during the night of fishing, the captain will go to bed, leaving the rig man in charge with his instructions. The captain's sleeping quarters are always behind and adjacent to the wheelhouse. Any time the nets are in the water, captains and rig men program themselves to sleep lightly. They will not allow themselves to relax. They must maintain a level of awareness and fast response.

They memorize the normal sound of the boat's engine and the winch when it is spooling and unspooling cables in and out of the water. They are able to sense and feel when the rig man is turning the boat around in the opposite direction.

They are able to feel if the boat is pulling more to one side, letting them know that there is something at the bottom of the Gulf that got lodged in one of the nets. They can distinguish the boat's bouncing, rolling movements caused by high seas from the resistance coming from the bottom of the sea. Any abnormal sound or sudden jerking movement stirs the captain, causing him to spring to his feet to assess the problem.

---

6   Shrimpers have a side-band radio on twenty-four/seven— listening to all communications coming over the air waves.

If the shrimp count is low (less than ten), the rig man continues the course ahead until the next try-net pick-up, hoping that the shrimp count will go up. If the shrimp count is higher than fifteen to twenty, they are coming up on an area at the bottom of the Gulf where there is more shrimp. The rig man lessens the interval of minutes in half before his next try-net check. If the shrimp count comes in higher than before (more than thirty), it is the place and time to fish.

THE SHRIMPING HEYDAY

Men who did not work on board boats, worked on land. Shrimp boats require lots of support personnel aside from the crew. Boats need engine mechanics, net makers, net menders, marine electricians, and ice house workers. Fish house dock workers unload the shrimp after a boat comes in with its ice storage bins filled with shrimp. You would think that these buildings would have been called shrimp houses, but they weren't. They were called fish houses. That's what they were called from the beginning and the name never changed.

The same happened when men were going out to sea to catch shrimp. The shrimpers, their families and everyone else in town would say that they were going fishing. That's what it was called in the beginning and that's what it's called today.

Other shrimp related jobs on land are shrimp processing workers. These jobs are filled mostly by women. They sort and box the shrimp according to size and quality. The bigger the shrimp, the higher the price paid for it. Men workers in these fish house/shrimp processing plants and freezers, store and freeze the shrimp, and load them into eighteen-wheeler refrigeration trucks to be transported to buyers in different parts of the country. The price of the shrimp is always set by the buyers. Demand and availability determines the price. The higher the availability of shrimp the lower the price. The lower the availability, the higher the price.

Many housewives take time away from their household chores to help fill the demand for workers during the initial peak days of the season. In those cases, the shrimp harvest is so lucrative that the boat crews can't keep up with the important job of heading the hundreds, or many times thousands, of pounds of shrimp caught during a single night of fishing.

Keep in mind that shrimp trawling nets take in everything in their path. These nets do not sort shrimp to one side, fish to another side, crabs to another. Everything goes in together. They start at the wide open mouth of the net. As the boat follows the course and speed set by the captain, its forward motion forces the catch further and further into the forty-foot-plus nets. Eventually everything ends up in the tail sack.

The first nights are always the busiest. Tons and tons of shrimp are typically caught during the first week of the season. The abundance of shrimp is so great that the captain determines how many times or for how long the nets will trawl for shrimp before bringing the next batch up for heading. There are anywhere from two to four drags (trawls) a night, depending on how many shrimp are being caught, and how fast the crew is able to head and ice them down.

Sometimes the quantity of caught shrimp is so great that the captain tells his crew to shovel as many heads-on shrimp as possible down into the ice storage bins. They ice down the shrimp and pack them until the bins are filled to capacity. To keep the shrimp from spoiling, the captain heads back to port full throttle. He radios in to the fish house office staff, telling them how many pounds of heads-on shrimp he that need to be unloaded, headed and sent to the processing plant for refrigeration ASAP! Shrimp with heads on spoil a lot faster than shrimp with heads off. The last thing a captain wants is for his entire catch to go bad. If that happens, he, his crew, and the boat's owner will make zero money, making the shrimp season a failure.

This is where housewives come into service. After getting the call from the captain that he is on his way, the entire fish house crew is put on alert. Orders are given to prepare to unload the shrimp as soon as possible. A fish house worker is sent out in a company pick-up truck to drive through all the neighborhood streets honking his truck horn. The horn is a notice to housewives that a shrimp boat is on its way with a hull filled with heads-on shrimp needing to be headed.

The housewives know where to report by the fish house pick-up truck and driver. Each fish house has its own truck color—and the same fish house worker is always sent out as the crier. This avoids any confusion and minimal loss of work reporting time.

The younger kids get involved too. Pre-teen boys considered too young or too small to go out and work as crew members on a boat hang around the docks belonging to different fish houses. There are always opportunities to earn a few nickels on the docks. They run errands for boat crews already moored and tied to the docks, waiting to unload or refuel or fill up with ice or working the nets and riggings getting them ready to go back out. The boys are used as runners. They run to the grocery store and bring back beer for the crew. They run to restaurants near the docks and come back with hamburgers. They run to other shrimp boats, fish houses, or net shops to relay messages. They run to different homes to relay messages to wives about one thing or another. They sweep and clean the boat cabin. All of these runner services are rewarded with a dollar or two by the end of the day and with soda pop, hamburgers—and often times a bread bag filled to the top with fresh shrimp to take home.

It doesn't take the housewives but a few minutes to get their gear ready and march off to the fish house calling them for duty. These mothers know that during the shrimp run they must have their shrimp heading utensils ready at all times. Heading tools consist of a kitchen boiling pot, latex gloves, an old dress and apron and old worn out tennis shoes and most importantly very fast hands. The faster the hands the more shrimp they head. The more shrimp they head the more money they earn.

Heading shrimp is a wet, dirty, stinky job. So the housewives make sure to dress accordingly. The boiling kitchen pot is placed right next to them so that they can put the heads in. They fill the pot all the way to the top first, before transferring and dumping the contents of shrimp heads into a bigger wash tub placed next to them by their feet. The wash tubs belong to the fish house and are placed there for them to fill. Once the wash tub is full, the women call out to workers to take the tub to the weight scale for weighing.

The mothers carrying their wash tubs filled with shrimp heads accompany the worker to the weigh station. The fish house foreman, usually the same person who drove the pick-up truck through the neighborhood calling them to come to work, acts as the weigh master. The office workers often double as record keepers and office secretaries.

As each tub is placed on the scale, the weigh master calls out the weight. The secretary writes it down on a carbon note pad and gives the woman a copy. The housewife either returns to her place at the shrimp-heading table and starts the heading process all over again, or she takes her ticket to the office and presents it for payment. Fish house headers are paid cash on the spot when the job is competed.

NIGHT LIGHTS OFFSHORE

Shrimper wives and the kids like to go to the beach after sunset to see the hundreds of bright, deck lights, floating all about like lighting bugs darting to and fro on the dark purple horizon. It seems as if hundreds and hundreds of twinkling stars have somehow decided to come down from heaven to swim, dip, and skip, as they frolic in the cool, refreshing waves of the Gulf of Mexico. These man-made stars can be seen flickering and gliding over the water as far off to the north of Padre Island's shoreline as the eye can see. Green, red and yellow lights brighten the night as boats sail slowly north and south. The ocean darkness behind them presents an all-black backdrop.

To the ever-vigilant captains, those entertaining lights represent maritime safety rules. The trawling direction, traffic movement and safe maneuvering of the fleet depend on those pretty lights.

Not all shrimpers fish the beach coast the first few nights. Many captains prefer to speed on ahead full throttle to their favorite fishing grounds—nautical miles and hours away from port.

Shrimpers who decide to fish close to shore for the first few nights do so for two reasons. One is to catch the abundance of shrimp that is still close to shore and has not migrated out to deeper water yet. The other reason is to test their boat's engine, winch, riggings, and other equipment. They don't want to navigate far out to sea for hours, perhaps days, only to travel back to port for repairs if some part of the boat breaks down. They will lose fishing time and lots of money. In shrimping, like all other businesses, "Time is money."

Offshore shrimping is a nocturnal job. There are several reasons why shrimpers lower their nets right at or right after sunset. Those who know say shrimp are nocturnal and come out only at night. That scientific explanation is hard to grasp. Since the bottom of the ocean is darker than night during day time as well as night time, how do the shrimp know when it's day time or night time? Others who also know say shrimpers shrimp at night because of the intense, punishing summer sun. Shrimp are delicate, susceptible creatures. They spoil rapidly if not iced down or refrigerated soon after they are caught and brought on deck. Shrimp go bad within a matter of a few hours. The freshness and preservation of fresh-caught shrimp is of utmost importance.

Shrimp boats line the Intercoastal Waterway throughout Port Isabel. Fleets are smaller today than in the industry's heyday, but the area is still recognized as the shrimping capital of the Gulf Coast—and in some cases arguably the world. Recent statistics show that the Port of Brownsville and Port Isabel are home to approximately 180 boats and still lead the state in shrimp production.

2

THE HISTORY

The Mexican fishermen of Port Isabel believe that the comic
old pelicans, that wobble like drunken sailors on the shores
of Laguna Madre and sun themselves on the white beaches of
Padre Island are the souls of drowned fishermen. The white
pelicans they believe to be the souls of good fishermen.
Port of Drifting Men by Leonard King

THE SEA, IT'S ALWAYS been about the sea. Whether in the Laguna Madre Bay or the Gulf of Mexico, Port Isabel residents have fished since recorded time. From the time when the Spanish explorers landed here through the present, fishing has been a primary part of the coastal experience.

Documents show that by the early 1500s, the Spanish found a safe harbor in the Laguna Madre where they traded their goods for dried fish. The indigenous tribes, who were hunters and gatherers, migrated through the area and played an important role in European settlement. The Comanche and Apache comprised most of the population.

The Spanish established their first government here in 1519 but it soon failed. However, they continued exploratory ventures and sought to establish local footholds. From about 1600 to 1700, the Spanish, French, English, Dutch and Portuguese all attempted colonization.

By the early 1800s, Port Isabel was becoming a major landing point. In 1826, the village opened the Main Customs House and cotton reigned as the number one export from the region.

Fishermen from La Pesca and Tampico, Mexico, came to Port Isabel because of its easy accessibility to the Gulf. La Pesca's inlets made it a prime fishing spot for trout, redfish, snook, oysters and shrimp. However, when the fish weren't biting at home, they migrated to Port Isabel. Likewise, Port Isabel fishermen would migrate to La Pesca at certain times of the year. Eventually many families from La Pesca stayed in Port Isabel and became important figures in the shrimping industry.

During the mid-1800s, Bagdad[1], on the south shore of the Rio Grande River became the largest port on the southwestern side of the Gulf. When the railroad opened between Brownsville and Port Isabel, the salted fish would be packed and sent to the Matamoros and Brownsville Saturday markets.

In the meantime, Richard King and Mifflin Kenedy settled in Brownsville and began working for Charles Stillman, the founder of the town and the owner of a riverboat company. The company made a lot of money during the Mexican-American War. After the war, Stillman formed a partnership with King and Kenedy. The company dominated the steamship trade on the Rio Grande River from the 1840s until after the Civil War.

---

1   There is a discrepancy in the spelling of this location. Mexico spells it Bagdad but the U.S. Drug Enforcement calls it Baghdad.

The lower Rio Grande Valley has known several names as well as flown several flags. The area south of Port Isabel to the Rio Grande and west to Los Fresnos was called the Jackass Prairie, so noted in several letters or diaries of soldiers in the Mexican American War. According to Mike Cateora, the area from the Rio Grande to Corpus Christi was known as the Wild Horse Desert. Both names refer to the wild horses and cattle that freely roamed the land.

By the 1920s, shrimping began to develop as an industry separate from fishing. Like the fish, the shrimp were cured in salted brine and put on rooftops to dry. Ice houses opened in Brownsville during this time. The ice arrived in Port Isabel by train, enabling fisherman to keep their products fresh longer. A little later, Harlingen opened an ice house.

The fishing and shrimping boats, typically fifteen-foot wooden skiffs, used five-foot sails. Every fishing family became boatwrights, borrowing money from the local commissary to build their own boat. Until this time, fishing had been mostly a barter business, trading their product locally as well as in Brownsville and Matamoros.

By the 1930s, shrimping was becoming a viable commodity but the market was poor. Fish brought more money. La Barra, the shrimpers' name for Padre Island, saw many boats along its shore every day.

In 1934, the fishing industry burgeoned with the success of the first Texas International Fishing Tournament in Port Isabel. The annual event is still a highlight of coastal fishing.

By 1936, the completion of the seventeen-mile-long channel from the Brazos Santiago Pass to Brownsville enabled the opening of the Port of Brownsville. It became vital to the shrimping industry and today is home to the Shrimp Basin. Driving down Hwy 48 to Brownsville, visitors can catch sight of the boat riggings and stop to buy fresh shrimp from the different shrimping companies.

World War II brought interesting changes to Port Isabel, not by shrimping, but by sightings of U-boats in the Gulf. Every time word arrived of the sinking of one of the U-boats, residents realized how close to home the war really was.

After World War II is really the beginning of the shrimping industry as we know it today. It is this period that is the focus of this book.

3

State of the Industry

Bumper sticker from Shrimp Outlet

"The old gray mare, she ain't what she used to be."
Lyrics from old folk song

BETWEEN THE 1940S AND 1980s shrimping dominated life in Port Isabel and the Port of Brownsville. Texas production grew to more than seventy million pounds of shrimp per year and a value of $143+ million. At its height, Texas consistently ranked with Louisiana and Alaska as the top three shrimping states.

Since the 1980s, shrimping has suffered a 70% decline. Texas boat licenses have dropped from 5,000 to 1,400.

When we asked shrimpers to define the reasons for the decline, they unanimously cited the same conditions. The Texas Shrimp Association gave the same reasons.

1. Government regulation

2. The industry has 13,500 regulations making it the seventh most regulated in the United States.

3. The cost of shrimp production has skyrocketed while the price of shrimp has remained level. Although shrimpers receive approximately the same revenue per pound, the cost of operation has tripled. Fuel is the major cost with a typical boat holding approximately 15,000 gallons of diesel fuel.

4. The government approved the importation of shrimp from other countries. While Americans consume a billion pounds of shrimp each year, the United States now allows 1.2 billion to be imported with little or no oversight. The major contributing countries include China, Ecuador, India, Indonesia, Mexico, Thailand and Vietnam.

5. Finding workers. Shrimping is hard and dangerous work. It is listed as the second most dangerous job in the country next to logging. A shrimper not only works hard, he is out to sea for months at a time, usually year round. The industry has depended on seasonal immigrant workers (mostly from Mexico) but Congress has limited the number of available visas. The shortage of workers keeps a number of boats idle at least part of the season.

6. Many shrimpers discouraged their sons from the lifestyle. Most of the men we interviewed wanted their children to have a better education and more opportunities.

On the other side of the coin, we asked about industry improvements.

1. Boats are safer. For example, railings that once were knee-high are now waist-high and the probability of falling overboard is greatly diminished.

2. Engines are more powerful and more fuel efficient.

3. Instrumentation and cell phones have improved both navigation and communication.

4. Synthetic nets have better webbing and are practically indestructible. They are stronger than steel.

5. Refrigeration changed the industry, allowing for longer fishing trips and better preservation of the shrimp.

Sammy Snodgrass believes there will always be a shrimping business. "But the industry is under tremendous pressure. Boats cost up towards a million dollars and gas and supplies cost more. Then there's the farm-raised and imported shrimp. Americans consume $1,500,000,000 pounds of shrimp a year. We're only producing $150,000,000."

The Statistics

National Oceanic and Atmospheric Administration (NOAA)

National Marine Fisheries Service (NMFS):

2016

$96.4 million: 38.3 million pounds—Brown shrimp

$54.3 million: 23.5 million pounds—White Shrimp

$ 5 million: 1.4 million pounds—Pink, Rock & Seabob Shrimp

2017

Fishery Management & Legislation

$6.5 billion in shrimp imported from 51 countries

90% Total U.S. consumption

⅔ of imports either peeled or cooked

(Exempts them from reporting law)

54% of imports from India and Indonesia

Only 4% of seafood imports tested for antibiotics

The Seafood Import Monitoring Program (SIMP) By NOOA Fisheries

SIMP established guidelines for the reporting and record keeping requirements for imported seafood products. Although the guidelines became effective January 2018, shrimp importers did not have to comply until the end of 2018.

Under the Fishery Management Act, Gulf of Mexico shrimp are safe, stocks are healthy, the industry is fully compliant and sustainable. Studies are conducted on an annual basis to assure continued compliance.

Shrimping facts according to the www.portof-brownsville.com in 2017

1. The port's fleet catches approximately 13 million pounds of shrimp each year with an estimated value of $72 million.

2. The local shrimp industry supports 1,400 jobs in Cameron County.

3. The entire Texas shrimping fleet consists of 550 vessels generating more than 45 million pounds of shrimp valued at over $274 million.

4. The industry supports approximately 5,000 jobs along the state's coastline.

4

A Modern Gulf Shrimp Boat

The biggest problem now is manpower. ~ Red Sagnes

IF YOU'VE EVER BITTEN into a scrumptious morsel of wild-caught Gulf shrimp, you have benefited from the back-breaking work necessary to bring it to your table. Not only is it hard work, it is dangerous and requires long periods of time away from home. It requires seven-day workweeks and at the height of the season, twenty-four-hours a day. It is mostly a solitary life, sharing cramped living quarters with the rest of the crew. The job offers no benefits and no retirement.

Today it is much less profitable even though the shrimp are more plentiful.

The Boat

Today's shrimp boats are steel-hulled, have refrigeration that allows for several months at sea, and range from sixty-five to ninety plus feet long. As working boats, every space has its purpose.

In Port Isabel's shrimping history, the boats changed from gas to diesel engines and from no ice, to ice and to refrigeration. While the boats improved in size and technology, some things didn't change. A boat is in constant motion and everything has to be secured. Motors remain loud and the crew can't escape fuel fumes.

Each boat is named, usually with two names, like the Bessie Mae or the Vera Cruz.

Jasper Bodden allowed us to board one of his boats, the Captain J, in dock between trips.

The cabin area is approximately twenty-eight feet long. It houses the stairs down to the engine room, the kitchen, the bunks, the captain's quarters, the head and the cockpit in the front houses the navigational aids.

The decks secure the winch and rigging when it is not in use. Access to the refrigeration unit is on the deck behind the equipment.

The following is a photo tour of the Captain J.

Entry to engine room.

Captain's Wheel

Bunk.

Hallway from cockpit to kitchen

The Winch.

The Rigging

The Crew

The captain is God. His word is law and he is responsible for all decisions. In reality, he is in partnership with the owner who provides the boat and gas. The captain manages everything else. He chooses his crew, acquires food and supplies, decides on the route, and determines the fishing grounds. He keeps in contact at all times with the owner and, if he is in a fleet, the other captains.

The crew typically consists of the captain, rig man and header. All but the header operate as independent contractors. The captain pays wages to the header based on work performed. After all expenses, he then splits the remainder with the rig man. That split varies from captain to captain, but typically ranges from forty to forty-five percent. They have no paid benefits and are responsible for their own tax records.

The rig man takes care of the rigging and the cooking. The lowering and raising on the nets, the repair of the nets and the equipment, and assisting the captain all fall under his job description.

The header helps the rig man with lowering and raising the nets, and is responsible for taking the heads off the shrimp. Speed and skill become his biggest assets. He also cleans—the decks, the nets, the kitchen and their quarters.

A shrimp has two horns, one on the head and the other on the tail. These horns are sharp enough to penetrate the latex gloves that the header wears. In addition, the trash in the nets—other fish and critters such as crabs—can cut and sting.

When the shrimp are plentiful, the team works together, doing whatever needs to be done to get the shrimp on the boat, headed and frozen.

The Fleet

Safety in numbers is a plus in many occupations. This is certainly true in shrimping. Although captains occasionally go out alone, they prefer to be part of a fleet. In case of engine problems or accidents, the boats help each other. The shrimpers shared several stories of men who fell overboard. The other boats immediately circled around and joined in the search for the missing man.

Since boats come and go within the fleet, when a boat is filled with shrimp, a captain will send his load back with a boat headed home or he will stop at a port and sell the shrimp.

Today plastic is used in the nets. In the early days when they were made of cotton, the weight became an issue when wet. Today's nets are much lighter and more durable.

When the nets are pulled, the shrimp and bycatch are dumped onto the deck. Crew members quickly sort through it and trash the bycatch. Then the heading of the shrimp begins. As they head each shrimp, it is thrown into a basket.

A shrimp basket holds seventy pounds. After the shrimp are headed, they are cleaned and packed in one-hundred pound crates, and placed in refrigerated storage. Once the boat is back in dock, the crew unloads the boxes and the owner takes over counting and weighing the boxes, and storing or distributing them.

At Zimco in Brownsville, I watched as the crew placed the boxes on a conveyor belt. Inside, people counted the boxes and loaded them first on a forklift and then onto a truck.

Unloading a boat at Zimco Marine

Placing shrimp baskets on conveyor

Shrimp packed, 100-pound per box, at Zimco Marine.

The Days of the Ice Boats

Ice allowed shrimpers to preserve the freshness of their catch and store it longer. However, loading and working with the ice presented a less-than-advancement to the crew.

Lanny Varnam explained how the boat pulled up to the dock where a machine loaded huge blocks of ice, about the size of a six-foot table top, into the deck. Then chippers break the ice into tiny shavings. The beauty of this pure ice soon changes as it is dumped into a large steel-lined open hole. Out to sea, once the shrimp have been headed, they are placed in buckets and handed down into the hole. A crew member rakes the ice over the shrimp. As the ice melts, it permeates the shrimp, keeping it cold for days. At regular intervals, the ice is raked and re-raked over the shrimp to cool it as long as possible.

The boat stops in various ports to unload and sell their catch. The ports typically included Galveston, Aransas, Arthur in Texas and Morgan City, Louisiana.

The Future

Port Isabel transitioned from a shrimp town to a tourist destination over the last twenty years. The many factors, from government regulations to Mexico's 200-mile international waters limit have lessened the Port Isabel and Brownsville advantage as a gateway to Mexico.

However, manpower remains the industry's biggest problem. Shrimp are still plentiful but too many boats sit idle because the owner can't find workers.

The future may depend on the U.S. Government's loosening of VISA restrictions and strengthening of control and regulation of imported shrimp.

Throughout history, there have always been men who thrive on life at sea. Of those we interviewed, all had that special light in their eyes when they spoke of the Gulf of Mexico, its beauty, its bounty, and its sometimes bizarre behavior.

5

FASCINATING FACTS WE LEARNED

The kettle in front of the Queen Isabella Inn is the only proven relic of the early railroad history of Port Isabel. People would seine the bay for fish, put them in brine-filled pots to preserve and then lay them out on rooftops to dry.

They became the first established fish traders. The train to Brownsville operated on Saturday and the fish would be packed up and sent to market.

What we know today as the Rio Grande Valley was once known as the Wild Horse Desert. Horses and cattle roamed freely from here to Corpus Christi.

In 1935, Carl Chilton from Brownsville played a key role in working with the Army Corps of Engineers to dig the Intercoastal Waterway. This waterway runs from Long Island in New York City to Long Island Village in Port Isabel.

During the mid-1800s, Bagdad (on the Mexican coast in what is now Matamoros) became a major port in the Gulf until it declined after the Civil War and was totally destroyed by hurricanes in the 1870s-1880s. The port played a major role in helping the Confederacy during the Civil War.

The boundaries of Matamoros extended to both sides of the Rio Grande River until the time of the Civil War. When hostilities broke out, those residents who felt allegiance to the United States moved north of the river to present-day Brownsville. Those with allegiance to the South moved south of the river.

Shrimping on the East Coast and the Eastern Gulf developed earlier than Texas coastal shrimping. According to Brendan Burke's paper, *Florida's Fleet: An Ebbtide of Shrimp Boats on the San Sebastian River*, "Shrimp boat building was a major industry during the 20th century on the city's (St. Augustine, FL) waterfront and between 1943-1985 almost three thousand, if not more, shrimp boats were launched by local builders."

It would not be until shrimpers from the Carolinas and Louisiana migrated to Texas in the 1940s-1950s that the beginnings of boat-building businesses sprang up in Port Isabel. Until then, most families built their own small boats.

The huge anchors that adorn many homes around Port Isabel came from Spanish galleons and pirate ships. According to Mike Cateora and Uvaldo Alaniz, the ships would anchor at the mouth of the Rio Grande. When they left, instead of pulling up the 2,000-pound anchor they tied a buoy on the anchor with chains (they didn't use ropes at that time) so they could find it when they returned. When the ships quit coming, the anchors remained at the bottom of the Gulf. Over the years, many have been brought up, but many more still remain.

During the late 1940s and early 1950s, shrimpers used a tickler chain. They lowered it in front of the net to make the shrimp jump up.

Shrimpers use their anchors to slow down the boat when they come through the jetties.

In 1990, the Lacey Act declared it unlawful to import, export, sell, acquire, or purchase fish, wildlife, or plants that are taken in foreign waters.

Shrimp is a luxury food. If people are having a hard time providing for their basic needs, they don't buy shrimp.

Imported shrimp are killing the domestic industry. Today, more than 1,500,000,000 pounds of shrimp come from other countries, primarily Asia, India and Vietnam. These shrimp do not have the rigid laws that control U.S. shrimp.

Shrimp spawn in the Gulf of Mexico. A female lays 100,000 to 1,000,000 eggs in the winter that hatch within the next twenty-four hours. By the time the larvae reach approximately one-fourth inch long, they are transparent. The winds and currents have taken them into the bay where they will feed and grow. Their growth depends on the warm bay waters. By spring they reach three-to-five inches in length and migrate back into the Gulf. If they survive, they may live up to two years.

Shrimpers fish for three species of shrimp; brown, white and pink. Brown shrimp make up about eighty percent of the Texas catch and are found out in the Gulf waters. White shrimp are found in the bay or close to the Gulf shore. Pink shrimp are found mostly in Florida and Mexico, but they are caught along the Texas coast as well.

6

THE PEOPLE

It's the quiet beauty of the sea that draws men to it.

MOST ARE OLD TODAY—MEN who have lived a life, or a significant portion of a life—at sea. They remember the beginnings, the small fishing village that became the shrimping capital of Texas. They can recall the locations of docks, fish houses, cantinas, restaurants and the streets where their buddies grew up. They tell stories of walking the dirt streets barefoot, running along the docks and their first times at sea. Some experienced sea sickness while others took to it like ducks to water. Some wanted life on the Gulf and others wanted to get out of town.

The older ones recall when the big boats from Louisiana first came to town. They remember the excitement of first trips into the deep waters of the Gulf. Smiles come to their faces when they talk about the days of growth, plentiful shrimp and work for everyone. They can summon memories at a moment's notice because shrimping's heyday was also Port Isabel's. Shrimping took the village from poverty to success, a time when every citizen benefited.

They love the sea and shrimping but readily acknowledge that it can be a rough and brutal way to make a living. None wished they had done anything else, but few wanted their sons to follow in their footsteps. A few captains, like Sandalio Alaniz, feel most at home when out to sea. Although he has loved the shrimping life, he's happy his children received an education and moved on to better opportunities.

Like all Americans, the shrimpers wanted a better life for their children. Port Isabel was a poor community and offered few career options other than fishing or shrimping. Many young boys quit school to help support their families. Others finished high school but were still expected to stay in the family business.

The few who bought fleets of boats and built successful businesses take pride in handing the family business down to their sons and daughters. They are the exception. Shrimping is still a man's world and the daughters are confined to administrative roles.

Port Isabel's population, primarily Mexican-Americans, hovered between fifteen-hundred and two-thousand in the late 1940s. After the war, shrimpers from Louisiana, Florida, and the Carolinas brought their families and, by 1950, the population exceeded twenty-three hundred. The influx of new families changed the demographics and, although the town remained mostly Mexican-American, European surnames became common.

Names from the early days are etched in people's minds, whether or not they're still actively shrimping. Any conversation will soon lead to Zimmerman, Boudreaux, Bodden, Burnell, Cuevas, Galloway, Snodgrass, Martinez, Varnam and many more.

7

SANDALIO ALANIZ

> Shrimping is brutal. I didn't want my kids to be shrimpers. But
> I love it.

Boat captains appreciated owners who supported and challenged them. A boat in good running condition with sufficient spare parts and working equipment made a hard life easier.

Fifty-plus years, a long time in any occupation! For Sandalio Alaniz, his whole life has revolved around shrimping. His dad, Sandalio Sr, and uncle, Uvaldo Alaniz, led the way. Sandalio and his brother, Jesus, worked every summer until they graduated from high school.

His father Sandalio Sr. grew up on a family ranch, a few miles from Port Isabel, on the Mexican side of the Rio Grande. Youngsters earned little money, or none at all, on Mexican ranches during the 1930s. Yet they were expected to work from sunrise to sunset with no questions asked. Sandalio Sr. had relatives in Port Isabel. Years earlier, these relatives left the ranch in Mexico and moved to Port Isabel in search of a better life. At least in Port Isabel they received an earned wage for a day's work. After working at several odd jobs, Sandalio Sr. signed on to work as a header on a shrimp boat. Through years of working as a shrimper, Sandalio Sr. worked his way up to rig man and eventually captain. This is when Sandalio Jr. first got the urge to be a shrimper. Like most young boys who grow up wanting to be like their fathers, Sandalio wanted to be a captain in charge of his own boat and crew.

Uvaldo Alaniz (L) and Sandalio Alaniz (R)

Sandalio followed in his father's footsteps. He grew up on the fish house docks of Port Isabel.

"The summer I was twelve, my dad gave me a choice. Work at my grandfather's ranch near Matamoros or go shrimping with him. I knew I wouldn't get paid at the ranch, so I chose shrimping."

The ranch was at least twenty miles from the nearest Mexican town of Matamoros. Once he got there he would be stuck there until his father came back a month or two later. The ranch had no electricity, running water and no TV. His grandparents had a radio, but because the radio operated on batteries and batteries cost money, they listened to it only for an hour or two in the evenings after supper. The radio station they listened to was in Matamoros, and of course, the music was in Spanish. Sandalio, raised in the U.S., was used to watching TV daily. He knew he would miss all of his shows. He liked Mexican singers and their songs because he grew up listening to them. His mother always had the radio on at home, tuned in to the local Spanish radio station, but he liked American pop music more. He and his siblings had their own radio and while his mother had her favorite station she listened to, the kids had their radio synchronized to the radio stations that played their favorite Motown, rock and pop music.

Sandalio loved the ranch and he loved his grandparents. When his father took him to visit his grandparents after a long shrimping trip, he found the days filled with fun and adventure. He got to run around the place virtually unrestrained, as his parents and grandparents spent their time visiting. These visits were all fun and games and that's how he wanted to keep them. So he chose to go shrimping. He knew that shrimpers ate well. Every time his father was planning his next fishing trip, he went to the grocery store to buy groceries for the crew. By the time he finished shopping, he had a train of shopping carts, loaded with all kinds of food.

Sandalio wanted to work for pay. He didn't know how much he would be paid but he would be happy with whatever he got, especially the food. So, his decision to go shrimping with his dad was an easy one for an all-American boy of twelve.

Thus began a career he still loves. It's the work, the call of the sea, the independence, the peace and the quiet. "Plus the pay can be really good," he added.

His first summer he earned twenty-five cents for every box of shrimp he headed. The trips which lasted seven-to-eight days netted him up to forty dollars. "At first, I only headed fifteen-to-twenty pounds each drag." He gave the money to his mother who either bought his clothes or saved it for him. He paid for his first bicycle.

"I got seasick the first three days, every trip. That seemed to last forever but I finally outgrew it." He spent the summers as a header until after high school graduation. He then became a rig man. "Rafael Garza was my first captain. I spent four years with him. Then in 1980, Bill Zimmerman gave me a chance as captain of the *Madera Cruz*. It was a steel-hulled, refrigerated boat. After a year, I moved up to the *Salinas Cruz*, which I captained for eight months. When a new boat, the *Plata Cruz*, was ready, I got it. I spent two years before getting the *Dorada Cruz*, which I captained for twenty years. It's great to get new boats but each time it's a lot of work. I had to set everything and mark the cables."

*The cables are marked by fathoms. Each mark has to be symmetrical to keep the boat level. Fifteen fathoms receive one mark, then every five-foot section increases. For example, twenty fathoms two marks, twenty-five three, and thirty four marks.

Land is noisy and it is difficult to adjust after months at sea. Sandalio hates the traffic and all the accompanying noise. "I love the sea, its comfort and its beauty. But it can be ugly, too."

Many of the shrimpers spoke of the adjustment needed to get their land legs after long times at sea. While working, their focus needs to be one-hundred percent on the job at hand. Otherwise, bad things happen—accidents and injuries. They understand and accept the need for total concentration.

"But sometimes the call of family can be stronger," Sandalio said. "I missed so much with my kids." Two of his children are December babies and he has never celebrated their birthdays with them. He missed school and sports events during the school year. The father of three sons and one daughter, he speaks of them with pride. "My wife, Betty, was in control of everything in our family. She took care of the kids, the money and our home. I think she's bored sometimes now that the kids are grown."

His boat, the *Moonglow*, belongs to Sammy Snodgrass. When he left here on January 6, 2018, it took him five days to get to Florida. During the trip, they fished every day. For Sandalio, a typical day at sea, when the shrimp are plentiful, consisted of one drag. The crew put the nets out around 11:00 pm and picked it up at 4:00 am. They dumped the shrimp out on the deck and the headers went to work.

One hundred boxes is considered a successful trip. On his recent Florida trip, Sandalio brought home four-hundred boxes, a giant haul by anyone's terms.

Every trip has its own set of problems. On one trip, he lost one of his headers in Florida because his Visa expired and he had to return to Mexico. He dropped him off in Ft. Myers. This increased the workload for the remaining crew members.

Sandalio remembered a trip in 1993 or 1994, when he thought he was outside the boundary for a sanctuary off the Florida coast but the Coast Guard stopped him. They took him into Key West, confiscated his shrimp and set a fine of $10,500. Eventually they lowered the fine to $5,500.

Captains have to remain diligent about legal and illegal boundaries. Most long-term shrimpers have stories about the scrapes with the Mexican authorities after the implementation of the 200-mile limit.

Captains learn by experience and Sandalio recalled several incidents. Once he wasn't paying attention when the wind came up. He didn't have time to make it to shore and needed to anchor the boat. He broke two anchor ropes (all they carried). The tropical storm passed over them, creating ten-to-fifteen foot waves. They spent all night in the Gulf within half a day from Port Aransas. Last year when he got caught in a storm, he went into Port Arthur to wait it out. When the waves were too high to see the jetties upon their return, they used the anchor to slow the boat and keep it from hitting the rocks.

He prizes his relationships with the boat owners and with his crew. He captained for Zimco for thirty-six years and has spent the last four years with Sammy Snodgrass. David Martinez, his rig man, has been with him for a year. "You have to respect your crew. No one can afford fights at sea." Like most captains, the search for headers can be difficult. He depends on Visa workers and experienced guys that like their job.

Sandalio is usually home about three weeks before he heads back out into the Gulf. "I just want to relax. The first couple of days are busy with boat things.

Then I have about a week before I start thinking about the next trip."

He hopes to work as a captain for four more years. Then he plans to trade his sea legs for full-time land legs.

8

UVALDO ALANIZ

> I virtually drowned at sea and I don't remember anything
> after my rescue.

AT EIGHTY-SIX, UVALDO ALANIZ is a pioneer in the Port Isabel shrimping industry. Although retired for many years, his memories of his life at sea remain fresh in his mind still today. During his career as a shrimper, he witnessed the beginnings of Gulf shrimping in Port Isabel. He came to Port Isabel as a young boy, in the mid-1940s. Before that he lived and worked on the family ranch on the Mexican side of the river, not far from Playa Bagdad. Though he grew up in Mexico, he was born in Brownsville, Texas. Back then it was common for pregnant women living in and around Matamoros, Mexico to come to Brownsville during the end of their pregnancy term to give birth. Most families on both sides of the border had relatives living here and there. Immigration and Border Patrol enforcement was more relaxed than.

People pretty much came and went as they pleased. Most people used the Brownsville International Bridge to come across for their daily or weekly business affairs in Brownsville like shopping, working or visiting friends and relatives. The same was true for people on the U.S. side. They came and went into Matamoros without any problem whatsoever. U.S. citizens especially loved going over to wine, dine, dance and shop at the Central Market Benito Juarez. Many people on the Mexican side of the river crossed over to the U.S. from where they lived. The lines at the bridge were often too long for their liking.

Uvaldo had aunts and uncles who lived in Port Isabel. His parents sent him over to live with them so that he could attend school in the U.S. or at least that was the pretense. There were no schools anywhere near their family ranch. More importantly. Uvaldo was about twelve years old when they sent him over. As far as his parents were concerned he was old enough to work.

He was enrolled in school but that didn't last long. A month or two maybe. School was not really the reason he came. He wanted to work with his uncles and other relatives fishing commercially in the Laguna Madre. When he turned fifteen, he got a job working as a header on a shrimp boat that fished out of the WBP fish house. (WBP is the acronym for White, Brown, and Pink, the three kinds of shrimp harvested from the Gulf of Mexico. Many people, if not most who have lived in Port Isabel, all of their lives never knew what WBP on the façade of the fish house stood for. Billy Holland, Mares Martinez and Uvaldo Alaniz all told us the meaning).

So at the tender age of fifteen, Uvaldo went to fish the Bay of Campeche. His age may have been tender, but he was not. He was already a hard-bodied worker with rough hands and strong muscles from working for three years on the bay.

He started as a header and earned one dollar per box. Working on ice boats, the average trip to Campeche was thirty-to-thirty-five days. He worked hard, learned well, was promoted to rig man and continued to fish Mexican waters. When he turned twenty, Martin Tower, owner of WBP, offered him a job as captain of the *Republic*. His brother, Sandalio Sr. worked as his rig man.

He saved his money and eventually bought his own shrimp boat, the *Robin*. After operating the *Robin* as owner and captain for a few years he bought his second boat, the *Adventure*. He renamed it the *Robin II*. Both were ice and wooden-hulled boats.

Uvaldo had an accident on board the *Robin*. He was sent to the seaman's hospital in Galveston, Texas for back surgery. Back in those days, shrimpers and all other Texas mariners received their hospitalization and medical care without out-of-pocket cost to them.

After he recovered from his first serious back injury, he had another bad fall. This time on the *Robin II*. Once again he needed back surgery. The second injury left him unable to shrimp anymore. He found it difficult to adjust to land after so many years at sea.

Uvaldo hired two captains to run his boats. Neither of them worked out. During his younger days as a shrimper and captain, Uvaldo was a hard person to work for. A perfectionist, he was driven and demanding of his crew. He wanted things to be done his way and according to his expectations. He had high performance standards and an exemplary work ethic. That's the way he was taught to work from a young age.

Needless to say, the captains he hired had a difficult time pleasing him. They didn't bring in the amount of shrimp he expected them to bring in, or they didn't take care of his boats as well as he did. He found out the captain of the *Robin* was stealing shrimp from him. He fired him. Disillusioned and discouraged that he was not going to be able to find trust-worthy captains who would take good care of the *Robin* and not steal from him, he decided to sell it.

He sold the boat to a lobster operation off the coast of Jamaica. Not long after he had sold the *Robin*, the captain of the *Robin* II tried to bring the boat in during a strong norther with gale force winds. He was not able to navigate and maneuver the rough battering wake and powerful currents that twist and churn in between the jetties during bad weather. He rammed into the jetties and the boat sank. Fortunately, the crew was recused by the Coast Guard.

He remembers when times were good for everyone in the shrimping industry. All of the shrimping related business both north and south of the border thrived. The money rolled in. Then the U.S. Government decided to establish and enforce the two-hundred-mile fishing limit. Things began to go bad for shrimpers. As time went on, conditions worsened. Additional government regulations like the TED slashed their profits even more. Fuel prices, insurance costs, supplies and all other expenditures spiraled. So things went from bad to worse, to terrible and finally to horrible. Small independent owners could not keep their heads above water. They went under. Shrimping in terms of high profits has not been the same since.

Despite his misfortunes during the later years of his shrimping career, Uvaldo had no regrets. He left the shrimping business and went into farming and ranching. He raised goats, sheep and cattle. He also farmed sorghum. His ranching and farming operation was south east of El Refugio, a small ranching and farming community about fifteen miles east of Matamoros along the Rio Grande.

The *Robin* II

He remembers the many Mexican ports he called on during his fishing days. His face lit up when he spoke of these ports. He had a sparkle in his eyes and a mischievous grin on his lips when he spoke of places like Isla de los Pajaros (Bird Island) an island on the south side of Tampico. He talked about Isla Lobos, Tuxpan, north of Tampico and the Port of Mexico, further south where the coast begins its turn to the east.

Although Uvaldo was never captured by the Mexican Coast Guard after they established the two-hundred-mile limit, he knew others who were. He shared the story of Captain Carlos Medina who worked for Zimco. He was chased and caught when a gun boat rammed the rear of his boat. The officers confiscated and towed his boat to Tampico. They took him to jail, where he spent the next twenty-nine days. After he paid the fine, he was released.

Whether talking about fishing the bay or venturing out into the Gulf of Mexico when the Louisiana fishermen came, he can talk about the differences between then and now. Before the days of Loran and GPS, fishermen used a compass measuring time and speed to create workable maps. Although the boats had a Fathometer, they didn't have the equipment to mark fishing locations. Crews carried pieces of foam (about two-by-two feet), bamboo sticks, small battery-operated lights, a small anchor and rope to identify good fishing spots. They would tie the light to the bamboo, which they stuck in the foam, and place it in the water with the anchor to hold it in place. These markers worked as buoys to guide the fishermen.

9

JOHNNY BARRIENTEZ

My dad started shrimping with no compass or other instrumentation on his boat.

THE CALENDAR MAY MARK Johnny Barrientez old at
eighty-six, but his enthusiasm for sharing a lifetime of
shrimping stories defies his age. He learned the trade
back when Port Isabel shrimpers fished only the bay
and along the shore off the beach of South Padre Island
and south towards the mouth of the Rio Grande. He is
one of the few remaining old timers who still remembers the beginnings of the shrimping boom.

At the tender age of six, he accompanied his dad,
Alfonso, out on his boat, *La Gaviota* (the Seagull). It
was one of the few boats that ferried passengers to and
from the island before the Queen Isabella Causeway
was built. Padre Island, as it was called back then, was
already a destination for beach and sun lovers. It may
not have been well known outside of the Rio Grande
Valley and Texas, but the Valley people loved it. They
had their very own paradise of clean pristine cool
turquoise water to frolic in during hot summer days.
Sports fishermen had an abundance of fighting tarpons

a mere hundred yards from land in the shallow flats of the Laguna Madre—red fish, trout, black drum galore! They had arguably the best tasting oysters anywhere. Port Isabel, Brownsville, the Valley and to some extent Texas people were virtually the only ones who were familiar with this small wonderland and fishing village.

Johnny was young, but he remembers the boat had lots of windows all along the front and sides. His dad was ready for a change in business. He was going to give fishing a try. He converted the *La Gaviota* into a shrimp boat. He had no instrumentation on the boat. He didn't need any. He began by fishing in the bay. There is no way you can get lost fishing in the Laguna Madre. You have Port Isabel to the west, Padre Island to the east, ranch land to the south and more ranch land to the north. You never lost sight of land.

Johnny recalled, "Back in those days we got our salt from what is now Long Island Village. After the *La Gaviota*, Dad started building a small shrimp boat, the *Dolores*. I think it was a twenty-five footer."

Port Isabel had a small, shallow channel on South Shore Drive. Johnny's dad Alfonso owned some property there. He built a small dock for his boats. The property now belongs to Jasper Bodden where he docks his shrimp boats.

The dredging and opening of the Brownsville Ship Channel brought new business opportunities to the Rio Grande Valley but more so to Port Isabel/Brownsville. Alfonso and Johnny extended their fishing grounds beyond the bay, past the jetties and into the Gulf of Mexico, close to shore.

They left the dock during pre-dawn. Because the ascending sun with its early morning glow was still minutes away from breaking the eastern horizon, they would set their early course east towards the guiding beacon of the lighthouse on the south end of Padre Island. The lighthouse stood twenty-five feet above the water, just north of the Brazos de Santiago Pass. They usually reached the Pass right about the same time the sun showed its golden crown. Depending on the wind speed and surf chop, Alfonso decided whether to turn south to the river or north along the shoreline to fish.

All the work was done manually. The only machine on board was a Model T gasoline Ford engine. The *Dolores* had a single rig, no winch, and no compass. The small nets were lowered and raised by ropes. An even smaller try net was lowered and pulled up every fifteen-to-twenty minutes. If twenty or thirty shrimp were in the try net, they would throw down a flag—a rope with a piece of cork with weighted metal—to serve as a buoy. This signaled other boats that shrimp were plentiful on that spot.

It took two men to haul in the nets, one on each side, taking turns pulling the ropes. Once they had the nets by the side of the boat, they tied them down to side posts. When the nets were full of shrimp and fish, they were too heavy to be lifted up on deck. They used long-handled dip nets to reach inside the net to scoop the shrimp out and dump them on deck. Once the net was light enough for them to lift, they brought it up on deck and shook out the rest of the catch. The boat didn't have ice and they didn't head the shrimp. They covered them with a large tarp and repeatedly soaked them down with water throughout the day. They fished until 4:00 in the afternoon, weather permitting, before heading back to dock.

When they reached a fish house owned by Pablo Valent, they unloaded the shrimp into big wooden tubs. Pablo had ice. He would process the shrimp, ice it down, load it onto trucks and transport it to Brownsville.

Johnny recalled a horrific accident that occurred to them during one of their fishing trips. The *Dolores* had a tragic explosion on board that destroyed the boat and nearly killed Alfonso. The boat carried a fifty-five-gallon gasoline tank on the prow of the boat.

To start the Model T engine someone had to go inside the small engine housing and crank the engine. Lorenzo, Alfonso's brother, remained outside on deck while Alfonso went inside the cabin. Alfonso noticed a leak in the gas line but he needed to start the motor. When he cranked it, a flashing spark shot off the spark plug and landed on the leaking gasoline. The line ignited and in an instant they had an explosion inside the cabin. Alfonso suffered serious burns over most of his body—miraculously, his stomach escaped the burns.

Fortunately, Lorenzo's quick thinking and fast reaction avoided a worse fate for them. He sprang into action. He ran to the fifty-five-gallon tank, yanked off the gas line and rolled the gasoline tank overboard. A sport fishing party was nearby. They heard and felt the loud, reverberating boom rush towards them over the water. Wasting no time, they motored over to the *Dolores* and its crew. On their way to the *Dolores* the sport boat captain radioed the Coast Guard.

When they got to the boat, it was in flames. As soon as the party boat pulled up next to them, Lorenzo grabbed Alfonso and jumped. When the Coast Guard arrived, they put the fire out but the *Dolores* was beyond saving.

"My dad didn't give up on shrimping. As soon as he healed from his burns he continued to fish." Johnny spoke with admiration for his father. Even after all these years, it's difficult to imagine the courage it took to survive the burns and return to shrimping. The brothers were strong, and that was the only life they knew. Once Alfonso could get up and around, he worked through the long recovery with most of his body bandaged.

They built a new boat, the *Santa Maria*. Greatly improved, it was powered by a new marine engine that had enough power to turn a small winch. Tiny by today's modern standards, the winch was less than twelve inches long and about three inches in diameter. A chain connected it to the motor, which had to be running for the winch to operate.

Johnny and his brother continued working with their dad. They never received pay but their dad provided for them. The *Santa Maria* was still one of only a few shrimping boats working the bay. They built a bigger second boat, the *La Nina*. She too had a bigger and more improved marine engine. However, neither boat had a compass, lights or any instrumentation. They never fished at night, only by day along the island shore.

A good day on the water produced approximately three baskets full of shrimp, each weighing somewhere around eighty pounds. That meant a catch of over two-hundred pounds of white shrimp, not headed.

Everything changed in 1941, after Pearl Harbor. Alfonso joined the Navy. Although the boys did their best to fill his shoes, while he was away at war, they were still children. Johnny became captain of the *Santa Maria* when he turned sixteen. Like most of us, he learned some lessons the hard way.

One day they had both boats fishing in front of Boca Chica Beach near the mouth of the Rio Grande River. A thick, heavy fog rolled in, catching them by surprise. Alfonso, who was on board *La Nina*, returned to port right away. Johnny mistakenly decided to stay behind and wait. He hoped the fog would lift after a while and he would be able to continue fishing. The fog gradually got thicker. They had zero visibility beyond the tip of the prow six feet away.

Instead of dropping anchor and waiting for the heavy fog to pass, he decided to head back to Port Isabel. "We moved at a snail's pace fearing that we would run the boat up on the beach. Uncle Lorenzo kept dropping a sinker in the water to determine the depth. He continued this as we slowly trekked north up the coast."

Finally, after what seemed like hours, they suddenly saw the jetty rocks right in front of them! Uncle Lorenzo yelled "Jetties, jetties, jetties." Johnny pulled back on the throttle and began to frantically spin the wheel to the right. He narrowly missed hitting the rocks. When he had the boat pointing east parallel with the jetty, he followed the rocks all the way to the end. Once he had cleared the rocks and rounded the point, he steered the boat to the middle of the channel, past the Brazos and into the Laguna Madre. They made it back to the dock safe and sound. They were exhausted but they were safe.

His dad's response, "You should have stayed out until the fog lifted."

Johnny always admired his dad's bravery. If the nets became entangled, Alfonso would jump in the shark-infested waters and untangle them. "He couldn't swim," Johnny recalled. He may have been scared of drowning, but he did what he had to do. He would go in the water because he was the captain. He felt that because it was his boat, he was responsible for everyone and everything on the boat. Not being able to swim was not going to put him in a position to order someone to jump in the Gulf water, risking their life to do repairs on his boat.

Johnny's mother died before his teenage years. He and his brother Jesus were assigned by their father to live with an aunt. In those days when a man became widowed, the responsibility of rearing the children was left up to a grandmother or an aunt, usually on the maternal side. Men supposedly were not psychologically adapted to raise kids. The sad and truthful fact is they did not want the responsibility.

More often than not the widowed man married again. The children from the first wife stayed with the grandmother or aunt. The father would began a new family. The few widowers who didn't remarry had to earn a living. Men in Port Isabel worked on the water. As a consequence, Johnny and Jesus lived their childhood years with relatives when their dad was out to sea.

After World War II, Alfonso came home with a new wife he met in Florida. They fell in love, married and he brought her to Port Isabel. He returned to shrimping.

Soon after the war, the big boats from Louisiana arrived. Johnny remembers the first time he saw one of these boats. It was named the *Alamo*. He is unable to recall the owner's name. The *Alamo* had a steel hull and bright lights all over the place. To his amazement, the *Alamo* had outriggers. One on each side like wings. Two big wooden doors dangled off each outrigger. Long iron chains and the biggest fishing nets he had ever seen were tethered to the doors. The winch was huge and so powerful that it was able to lift and drop the two outriggers along with all of their attachments with ease.

In 1951, Johnny graduated from high school and joined the Marines. He and four of his high school buddies joined together. Fortunately, all five friends returned home alive after their service. Johnny spent a year in Korea during the Korean War. After his tour of duty in the war, he was stationed at Camp Pendleton in California. There he met Mary Ann and they married in 1953. After his discharge, he and Mary Ann came back home to live. He looked for work but he wasn't able to get the type of job he wanted. They moved back to California, where he still lives.

Jesus became an electrician. Lorenzo continued shrimping.

10

JASPER BODDEN

> Shrimping gave me a good life.

JASPER'S READY SMILE AND reticent manner don't fool the observer. As a man who has spent fifty-six years of his life shrimping, he knows the industry inside and out. He's lived through the good times and the bad. Jasper immigrated from Spanish Honduras when he was nineteen. He was seventy-five at the time of our interview. He has spent all the intervening years learning shrimping from the bottom up.

His parents owned a ranch in Honduras and as a young man he knew he didn't want to spend his life on the land. The call of the sea led him to Port Isabel where he first worked as a header on the *Sea Garden*, owned by David Cox. After five months, he became a rig man and held that position for the next five years.

In 1962, he became captain of a sixty-two-foot, steel-hulled boat. Two years later he captained a new boat, the *Maria G*.

"It would take us about fifty-four hours to get to Campeche. We would fish for fifteen days and then send the shrimp back to port. The boats were all ice back then," Jasper recalled. "I bought my first boat in 1970, for $90,000."

Jasper's business grew in the 1970s. At the height of his career, he owned thirteen boats. When Mexico closed its coast, fishing changed for U.S. shrimpers. The abundant waters that had carried them through the winter seasons were now off limits. Like many of his peers, he had some problems with Mexico as a result of the new rules.

"I had two boats seized by Mexico in the 1970s. By the time I paid the fine and refitted the boat, it costs me $54,000 to get one back."

Jasper has six boats today. His main problem now is personnel. "We bring in more shrimp per boat today, but it's a challenge to find people to work."

Like all the shrimpers we interviewed, Jasper loves shrimp.

11

WALLACE BOUDREAUX

1923–2016

ALTHOUGH WALLACE PASSED AWAY in 2016, his accomplishments live on in the shrimping community. His memory looms large and all the shrimpers we interviewed spoke of his contributions to the industry and Port Isabel.

Born in Louisiana in 1923, he started shrimping at the age of fifteen and was in his mid-twenties when he moved to Texas. He bought his home in Brownsville and established his business in Port Isabel. According to Red Sagnes, he faithfully drove back and forth every day. "He couldn't read or write. If he needed something read, he'd hand it to me to read for him. He was very smart, remembered everything, every detail." Wallace became one of the most successful men in the business.

He was a founding member of the Twin City Co-op and later owned Twin City Shrimp Co.

A man of faith, he belonged to Sacred Heart Church in Brownsville, where he attended Mass every Sunday.

As a boy he also learned farming with his family, using mule-driven equipment. He worked hard his entire life and garnered the respect of his peers. However, he brooked no nonsense in his employees. Red recalled a time when he was waiting on a header to go out on the *Louise L.* The guy refused to leave the bar. Wallace physically drug him to the boat. In his drunkenness, the man fell overboard as they were leaving the dock. Wallace fished him out of the water and headed to Campeche with him on board.

Wallace enjoyed interacting with his crew and when they returned home, he'd drink a beer with them. "Only one though," Red said.

He owned four boats—the *Captain Wallace B*, the *Mr. Webb*, the *Mary Kalei* and the *Cathy Ann.*

Rudy spent a summer on the *Louise L* when he was
first married

12

CHARLES BURNELL

> The shrimping industry won't last more than five years if they don't regulate imports.

CHARLES BURNELL IS A man of many quotable phrases. His many years in the shrimping industry have given him insight into the business and its people. He is a second-generation shrimper, and his son Kiel (pronounced Kyle) now works with him.

In 1928, his dad came to Port Isabel to work on the dredging of the fingers (a series of canals connecting homes to the bay). During the Great Depression of the 1930s, he started fishing and selling his catch. At that time, fishermen used little (thirty-to-thirty-five foot) gas boats. Every year, one or two would blow up at the docks.

During the 1930s and 1940s, the nets were made of cotton. The boats didn't have a winch and the nets had to be pulled in by hand. After WWII, the fishermen began installing winches.

His dad, B.B. Burnell, served as the Port Isabel mayor from 1941–1945. A well-loved public official and also an avid hunter, he sponsored a citywide barbecue each year. Everybody in town joined in the annual celebration. As a kid, Charles remembers softball games and fish fries.

In his 1945 saga of Port Isabel, *Port of Drifting Men*, Leonard King described the town and its inhabitants during the 1940s. "Burney's appetite and courage is matched only by his fortitude and honesty."

B.B. bought about three-quarters of the South Shore dock area in Port Isabel for $7,500. In 1946, he built the WPB building (then named Burnell Fish House) to capitalize on the burgeoning shrimp industry. He started buying shrimp, which was mostly the white.

As a boy, Charles would go out fishing during the summers. He made eighteen dollars his first year. It was enough to buy his clothes for the following year. By the time Charles graduated from high school in 1951, shrimping had become a thriving concern. At the fish house, his dad set up header trays. When a boat returned home, he would blow a siren and every able-bodied person in town came to head the shrimp.

In 1962, Charles became a captain. His brother-in-law followed in 1964. Their boat, *Blood & Guts*, made the Associated Press news in 1972. They were running fifteen miles offshore on a black night when the Mexican Coast Guard fired upon them, boarded and confiscated the boat and hauled Charles off to jail. While there, he had to pay for his own meals.

After four days, they released him. The third day, an article in the local paper announced his coming release. Everyone else knew he would get out but he didn't understand Spanish so he didn't know. They set the bail at $1,400. He paid the fine but the "illegal waters" charge was disputed by the US.

"Every time Mexico took a boat, they raised the fine," Charles recalled. It's the kind of story that many shrimpers experienced over the years. It became even more frequent after the 200-mile limit was established.

"I had a dog named Partner that always went on the boat with me. Once when a storm came up, I told the crew to go below and take the dog. One of the crew members mumbled to the other, "That damn, no-good captain thinks more of that dog than the crew." Charles gets a good chuckle out of retelling that story.

Another time, Partner jumped up on the net and it flipped him out in the water. Charles wanted to go in after him. "No, you're not. No, you're not," his rig man insisted. Then he pulled off his pants and dove in after the dog. All Charles remembers is that his rig man was wearing shorts with red hearts.

Charles fished the entire Gulf and never waited for others to join him. Although most shrimpers find safety in fleets, he would take his boat out alone. Sometimes his bravery edged toward foolishness. One time out alone, a southeast wind came up and his loaded boat took two strong waves. "I should have slowed down," he admitted.

In 1967, he was off the Galveston coast when Hurricane Beulah arrived. He headed home, keeping his eye on the long, lazy ground swells. By the time he reached the jetties, there were sixteen-foot seas. He had to go back to Port Lavaca to unload the 13,600 pounds of shrimp. Since he was on an ice boat, he only had thirty-six hours.

On a return trip from Louisiana, he noticed a big black cloud. A friend ran his boat down and warned him to turn around. When he turned around, he was only about a mile from the biggest funnel he ever saw. He estimated it measured 400–500' wide.

Charles believes the industry runs in seven-year cycles. When he and his brother-in-law started out in the early 1950s, they made $1,100 in six weeks. It was enough to pay for a year at Texas A&M. In 1962, he made $8,000 and dropped out of college.

"Port Isabel is the front door to Mexico," he said. That accounted for its tremendous growth during the 1950s. "When Mexico shut down (establishing the 200-mile limit in 1976), it pretty well killed Port Isabel shrimping. Now the majority of shrimp are caught closer to Galveston."

Charles owned fourteen boats at one time. He is now down to six. "At one time there were 400 boats in Brownsville, now just over 100. Port Isabel had 250 boats and now only about fifty."

He believes that trust is key to running his business. Charles has to constantly be on guard against theft. Owners experience it all—the captain that pulls into a port and sells shrimp or the crew member that messes up the motor so the boat has to head to a port. Years ago, owners had a big problem with tourists. They wanted to buy shrimp directly off the boat. Unfortunately, many times the crew would trade shrimp for beer. A good deal for the tourists who received $100 worth of shrimp for $20 worth of beer. A bad deal for the owners.

Sometimes owners try to cheat the captain, knocking down the amount brought in. Charles believes that if you steal from them, they'll steal from you.

13

MIKE CATEORA

> To understand the shrimping boom, you have to understand
> Port Isabel history.

DESCENDED FROM A PIONEER fishing family, Mike
is an expert on Port Isabel and Rio Grande Valley history. Mike's grandfather fished for a living in the early

1900s. Like most merchants, he had a wooden skiff with gill nets, which were later banned. They would have depleted the fish. The gill nets hung vertically in the water and trapped everything that swam by. They entangled fish by their gills and damaged every form of wildlife.

In the mid-1920s, he migrated to La Pesca every winter. Fishermen salted their catch in wooden barrels and took them to the Monterrey and Tampico markets. At that time, little money exchanged hands. The fishermen bartered and traded their product for needed supplies such as flour, sugar, and coffee.

World War II deterred the shrimp industry. The boats ran on kerosene, which was in short supply, and many of the shrimpers served in the Armed Forces.

When the shrimp industry took hold in Port Isabel, he opened Brazos Fisheries. The only other fish house in town belonged to Charles Burnell. At Brazos, he focused on finding a market for the shrimp and serving the production needs of the industry.

To prepare the shrimp for shipping, they were packed in five-pound boxes, ten to a carton. This system is still used today.

White shrimp brought the highest money per pound. They could only be caught in the daytime and shrimping became known as a "ghost industry." The brown shrimp, though plentiful and a nighttime catch, were a much more difficult sell. The pink shrimp found in Mexico and Florida fared better. Pink are the only shrimp that can be caught any time of day.

Mike was born in Port Isabel. Like other boys, he learned shrimping as a boy. He attended Pan American University, but did not graduate. Like his grandfather and father, he became a shrimper. He captained a boat for a few years. He recalled some of the boats he worked on: the *Chapala*, the *Acapulco*, the *Miss Ruth*, the *Henry* and the *Miss Beulah*.

Over the years his family had been in the business, the industry grew by leaps and bounds. Modernization changed everything. His grandfather fished in a twenty-six-foot wooden boat, the first one built in Port Isabel. Today's boats average seventy-eight to ninety feet with steel hulls.

Mike's love of Port Isabel and its history led him to become an expert local historian. He's the kind of storyteller who can weave an area's documented history into accounts of local legends and interesting tidbits.

The demand for shrimp led the influx of shrimpers from other states. The brown shrimp of the western Gulf waters were different and the demand was low. In the beginning, the fish houses shipped their products to Fulton Fish Market in New Jersey. In some cases, they had to give it away to educate people.

By the early 1950s, French, Cajun, Portuguese and Italian shrimpers all brought their hopes and dreams to Port Isabel. Hundreds of boats lined the waterway.

Once shrimping hit its peak in the 1950s to the 1970s, Texas shrimpers became concerned about the preservation of shrimp. They collectively petitioned the Texas Parks and Wildlife to establish a season that gave shrimp time to grow and mature.

At one time, nearly eight hundred shrimp boats were in operation. Port Isabel ran out of room and discontinued dock rentals. Owners moved to the larger Shrimp Basin at the Port of Brownsville.

14

PEPE AND EJ CUEVAS

> Four Generations of Shrimpers
> The Cuevas Family

Pepe and his grandson EJ

IT STARTED MORE THAN fifty years ago. Francisco "Chico" Espinosa took his son "Pepe" (Jose) with him one summer day to the WBP Fish House dock. Pepe was a boy not yet ten years old. Chico worked as the dock foreman for the company. He managed a crew of a dozen or so men depending on the demand of the season. His was one of the most important jobs in Port Isabel. Everyone in town knew and respected Chico. He hired and fired people, but mostly he hired.

The owners of WBP respected and valued Chico. A natural leader, he had a knack for managing men, especially dock workers. Because of his supervisory skills, the owners did not have to worry about the dock operations. Chico ran a tight and efficient outfit. They had great confidence in him. They did not have to spend their time overseeing dock happenings.

Dock workers are robust, brawny, hard men that are difficult to manage. Chico was not a large man physically, measuring perhaps five feet, five inches in height. Hence his nick name "Chico" which means small in size, or in barrio terms young small boy. What Chico lacked in size, he made up in strength of character and personality. He knew just how to handle and lead Mexiquito's men, young and old.

He had a hierarchy system of running things. Directly under him he hired local Mexiquito patriarchal men and gave them authority over their crew. These head of family clans knew how to control their underlings (mostly direct family members). Most had little formal education but they somehow knew (usually by alpha dominance) how to gain and maintain loyalty from the family.

Chico was a WWII veteran. Perhaps his time in the military and war gave him the skills to command men. Whatever the reason, captains liked him because he always loaded and unloaded their boats in an orderly and timely manner. He was well-organized and adept at moving and rotating the boats for fueling, icing and prepping for the next fishing trip.

Pepe grew up working for his father. As a dock worker, he saw shrimp boats lined up one behind the other, being unloaded with thousands of pounds of shrimp. He saw and heard happy shrimpers boasting of great fishing spot finds. What he liked and admired most about these men was listening to the fantastic sea stories and adventurous tales they spun of ports of call. However, these stories were never told nor spoken of beyond the dock or dock side cantinas and bars. They were meant for the ears of other shrimpers only.

Wives' and daughters' tender and delicate ears were spared any mention of the respite rendezvous and visits to taverns, cantinas, and public houses in these ports away from home.

Pepe also liked the money they earned. So at thirteen he decided he was not going to attend school any more. He got a job on a shrimp boat. He was ready to join the fraternal brotherhood of shrimpers. As all shrimpers do, he started at the bottom rung as a header. He headed shrimp for years (from age thirteen to twenty). He then became a rig man. All the time he rigged, he made and kept mental notes of everything having to do with shrimping. He especially kept notes of all the different fishing grounds.

When he finally worked his way up to captain, Pepe had amassed a great deal of knowledge in regards to shrimping. His wife Trinidad "Trine," like all other wives, managed the house, the finances and the children's welfare. They worked together as a team—Pepe as a successful captain and Trine as a faithful wife and mother.

They saved their money and eventually bought their first boat. Pepe continued fishing and Trine continued saving money. They bought a second boat, then a third, a fourth, a fifth, and they kept making and saving money and buying more shrimp boats until they owned eleven boats. They also invested in real estate property. Today Pepe is the biggest shrimp boat fleet owner in Port Isabel.

It wasn't easy for him and Trine. All shrimpers go through hard times. Pepe was caught fishing in Mexican waters three different times. He spent days and weeks in Mexican jails in Tuxpan and Tampico. He paid hefty fines and lost lots of money as a consequence. Shrimping is all that Pepe knows. His hard work and the Gulf of Mexico have paid off and been good for him.

He no longer goes out on his boats. Pepe is in his seventies. He still goes to the dock every day and manages his boats. All of his children are involved in the business.

His son Edward is a captain. Another son Pepe Jr. owns and operates a sea food market and restaurant where they sell and serve the freshest and tastiest shrimp. His daughter Inez, now deceased, took care of the company books and was also a boat owner. His wife Trine worked in the company office helping with the bookkeeping. His grandson E.J. (Edward Jr.) works for him on the dock and owns two shrimp boats of his own.

Pepe still calls all the shots and makes all of the decisions. As far as he and all of the children are concerned, he is still in charge. He is longer a boat captain. However, he is in fact an Admiral of his very own shrimping fleet.

15

VONCILLE GALLOWAY ZAMA
THE GALLOWAY FAMILY

Everyone is Port Isabel knew each other. All of our families were involved with shrimping.

Voncille in front of her artwork at the Laguna Madre Art Gallery

VONCILLE GALLOWAY ZAMA CAME to Port Isabel as a child in 1947. Her father, Alvah T. Galloway, had moved the family from North Carolina to Louisiana, before her birth. Together with Wallace Boudreaux, they built the Twin City Co-operative Association in Morgan City, their hometown.

Alvah T. Galloway

In 1949, the two opened Twin City Co-op in Port Isabel. Other shrimpers joined the co-op but Alvah and Wallace continued to own the majority shares. Alvah served as president for many years. His wife did the company's bookwork.

Voncille's many memories of growing up in Port Isabel include the joys of small-town life. She came to town with ready-made friends from other Louisiana shrimping families. Once here, she soon developed new friendships. "Everyone was friendly and we all played together. It didn't make any difference what your dad did, the whole town was involved in shrimping in one way or another. The only difference between the locals and those of us from Louisiana was our religion. Most of the natives were Catholic and we were Protestant."

Her older brother, Elmer, had an accident when Voncille was ten. He told her she had to learn to drive to run errands for the family. "That's the way it was back then. I drove because I needed to."

"Dad never owned more than two or three boats at a time. He made a good living and that was all he wanted." All of their boats were black and white and several bore the name *Voncille* or *Miss Voncille*. Both of Voncille's brothers were active shrimpers.

She graduated from Port Isabel High School at the age of sixteen. She had already met and fallen in love with Rob Zama. He was stationed in the Air Force in Harlingen. After graduation, she attended business school in Houston. In 1957, Rob received orders to move to Portland, Oregon. He asked her to go with him. She needed her parents' permission to get married because she was only seventeen.

In the early 1960s, she and Rob bought their first shrimp boat, the *Cindy Lynn*, in Louisiana and joined the Twin City Co-op. He didn't like the business and they sold it. But in 1972, when Alvah passed, she inherited the *Georgia Lady*. Her brother, Elmer, inherited the *Miss Voncille*. Their mother turned the business over to Jimmy (Alvah III).

While they owned her, the *Cindy Lynn* played an important role in the industry. The IRS and shrimpers were at odds concerning the payment of withholding tax. The IRS determined that crew members were employees and owners were required to pay withholding. The owners fought against this declaration, stating that crew members were self-employed, working as independent contractors and, therefore, responsible for their own taxes. Alvah went to Washington D.C. to argue the shrimpers' case. He used the history of the *Cindy Lynn* crews to verify the shrimpers' argument. The industry won and owners continued to pay the captains a percentage of the catch.

When the industry slowed and the Twin City Co-op fell apart, Alvah and Wallace retained the property. When they later had a disagreement, they split up and divided the property. Alvah moved his operation and Wallace kept the original location.

After seventy years of living in Port Isabel, Voncille and Rob made the decision to move back to Morgan City to be closer to their children and grandchildren.

16

BILLY HOLLAND

> I kept my kids away from the boats. I didn't want them to be shrimpers.

AT SEVENTY-NINE, BILLY HOLLAND has a long, rich history of Gulf shrimping.

"I've been shrimping since I was fourteen," he said. "It was in the early 1950s and the first boat was the *Cartagena*, owned by Mike Cateora's grandfather. It was a fifty-foot boat with a single rig and a small engine."

The two-man team, the captain and Billy, fished twenty miles off the jetties and would stay out for two or three days at a time. They fished in the daytime for white shrimp and would anchor out at night. They iced the shrimp and brought them back to the fish house to be headed. Their catch averaged 300 pounds.

"I left school because I had to work. My mother worked as a housekeeper at the Port Isabel Yacht Club. My father died when I was four. I had three brothers and one sister." Billy remembered how hard his mother worked to support the family.

The shrimpers from Louisiana and North Carolina arrived in the 1940s and 1950s with bigger boats and lights for night fishing. His first job on the bigger boat was on the *Sherry Anne*, a sixty-foot ice boat. They started night fishing for brown shrimp and stayed out ten-to-fifteen days. They averaged 1,000-pound loads. Shrimp was selling for thirty cents a pound and the crew received fifty percent of the take.

Billy started as a header. He worked his way up to rig man and became a captain when he was eighteen. His first boat as captain was the *Debra Kay*, owned by Twin City. They averaged seventy-to-eighty-thousand pounds per trip. According to Billy's memories, the market price for brown shrimp was two dollars per pound. The crew received forty percent. The header received a set fee per pound and Billy split the profit fifty-five for him and forty-five to the rig man.

In the 1960s, his family bought their first boat, a sixty-foot wooden hull boat. The boat, owner-financed by Towers, cost $40,000. His brother served as captain. Billy was in his mid-twenties.

They later sold that boat and bought the *Davy Crockett*, a sixty-eight-foot, steel-hulled ice boat. Merchants Marine Bank financed the $70,000 purchase.

About five years later, another brother, Gonzalo, bought his own boat, the *Miss Valerie*, a sixty-two-foot, wooden-hulled boat.

Billy became captain of their next purchase, the *L'il Lamb*, a sixty-five-foot, steel-hulled boat from WBP (owned by Towers). He owned the boat for thirty years. In 1972, he converted to refrigeration which enabled him to stay out to sea for thirty-to-sixty days.

Like other shrimpers, in the winter he fished the Bay of Campeche in Mexico. The trip down took sixty hours. Once there, the clear water was a gold mine of mostly pink shrimp. He was usually there from October through January, missing the holiday season with his family. The fishing in Campeche ended in 1980 when the international line was extended to two hundred miles.

Billy was caught fishing in Mexican waters. He had a boat filled with shrimp and three red snappers. The snappers were illegal. The U.S. Coast Guard charged him with smuggling. The Mexicans fined him $5,000 and confiscated his boat and shrimp. He hired an attorney who negotiated a lesser U.S. charge of illegal shrimping. He received a two-year suspended sentence.

He also fished off Veracruz where brown shrimp were plentiful. The Mexican Coast Guard caught him fishing one mile inside the limit. They again confiscated his boat for ten days and stripped it of equipment, supplies and shrimp. He spent one day in jail and was released after paying the city and county judges. He received a $10,000 fine.

On another occasion, when he was fishing close to the International limit, a Mexican gun boat shot at him with a .50 caliber gun. He headed toward shore all the way to the river, with the Mexican boat following and intermittently shooting at him.

> I credit my wife one-hundred percent for keeping our family together and raising our kids.

Billy readily acknowledged the role his wife played in his success as a shrimper. She accepted the lifestyle and "did a marvelous job." He knew it was hard for her but he could work away from home for seven months each year and rest assured that everything was fine in her hands. He wanted his children to get a good education and kept his boys away from shrimping. Every summer he planned a family vacation.

"Sometimes crew members got paid and spent their money drinking. I always made a point to spend time at home with my kids." Today he's proud of his children and feels they have successful lives.

Billy quit shrimping when he reached seventy. "It was a good life. I was rewarded financially and my kids did fine." Billy made a good living during his lifetime but he worries about today's shrimpers.

"People can still get good catches now but the cost keeps going up and the price of foreign shrimp goes down. I finally let my boat go because I had too much trouble finding a crew. In the beginning I could find plenty of workers from Port Isabel but not anymore." He said a number of boats are tied up this year for that reason. They can't find local workers and the visa cap has curtailed the Mexican workers.

When asked about the future, Billy believes it's not bright. His reasons are the common ones—high fuel cost and low-cost imported shrimp.

Sharing stories—yes, sometimes fish stories—is a common pastime among the shrimpers. Billy talked of friends who misjudged the entrance to the jetties when returning home, missing them completely and running their boats on the beach. Sometimes they ran aground because the fog was so thick they could not see their hands in front of their faces. Other times tempest storm waves were too high, covering the jetties. They didn't know if they were coming in north or south of the rocks. Still other times they wrecked their boats right on top of the jetties. Strong gusting winds and whirling currents were simply too hazardous for them to navigate.

He recalled losing a friend and fellow captain, Juan Castillo, who fell overboard and was never found. It's not uncommon for men to fall overboard during a storm, usually off the back deck, but in most cases, due to the quick thinking and response time of the crew, they are recovered. His brother Gonzalo was wearing his life jacket when he fell overboard. Wearing life jackets is not a common thing among shrimpers—either because they are too confining or because shrimpers are prideful men and wearing a life jacket gives the appearance of being timid and afraid.

While trawling, Billy has made some interesting catches. One time about ten hours out from the jetties, they netted rolls and rolls of material he had never seen before. It took them hours to remove the fabric from their nets, resetting them and rigging them back for the next trawl. They lost a lot of time and money. Another time while fishing off Veracruz, they brought up an Aztec artifact. It was a large heavy, carved head stone memorializing some ancient native God to the Aztecs. When they went into port to show their find to the Mexican officials, they of course kept it. Mexico said it was a National treasure and they had all the rights to it. However, the Veracruz government confiscated it.

Another time he trawled up an old rusted safe. They thought that perhaps they had found a sunken Spanish treasure. The crew thought that they were all going to be rich. They were certain the safe contained millions of dollars of Spanish gold and silver. They worked excitedly for hours trying to pry the box open, all the while talking about what they were going to do with their share of the booty. One was going to build a big mansion with lots of servants and retire in luxury. Another was going to buy a fleet of shrimp boats and live like the rich boat owners live. Yet another was going to make everyone in his family rich, buy a ranch and orchards in Bayview and live as a country squire.

After taking turns hammering the chest with the biggest crow bar they had on deck, they finally smashed the treasure chest open. Once the hinges and the lock were taken off, they stood silent for a short while before looking inside. Captain Billy had the honors of poking his head inside to look at their wealthy dreams. He took the crow bar with great expectations and poked at the contents. All he found, much to everyone's disappointment, was a bunch of broken, shattered, porcelain plates and cups. Their illusions of grandeur were swept away by the sea breeze. They were left with sore arms and a rusted broken iron safe and nothing but broken dreams. They each smoked a cigarette, then tied the box up with ropes and threw it overboard to sink back to the bottom of the Gulf from where it came. They shook it off, fixed their riggings again and went back to work—puffing out silver smoke rings and watching them drift away into the trade winds.

Storms offer unique challenges. Billy and his brother Gonzalo encountered a storm with forty-to-fifty mile-per-hour winds. As they battled the fierce tempest, they maneuvered their boat into the giant, white-capped waves. They pulled back and forth on the throttle, as the prow of their boat ascended almost at a thirty-to-thirty-five-degree angle before plunging back down between two fifteen-foot-tall waves. All of sudden, a twenty-five-foot-high rogue wave crashed violently, charging at them. Gonzalo, who was at the wheel, froze in disbelief at the sight of such a monstrous wave. He failed to pull back on the throttle. "The boat shot straight up and went airborne, flying in mid-air for a couple of seconds. When gravity pulled us back down, the next giant wave hit us mercilessly head on. The impact of the next wave was so brutal that it smashed the front windows. The wrecking wave was so powerful it sent us tumbling haplessly about the wheelhouse."

Billy shared the following story:

"By the time we regained our senses, the wheel of the boat was spinning out of control to the right and to the left and the boat was reeling. The waves kept pounding us every which way. We were doomed. Or so it seemed. We kept trying to hook the twirling wheel with the pilot ropes. We finally hooked one side, then the next. After much expended adrenaline, we were able to straighten the boat back into the fronting storm. Hours later after tempest winds and damaging waves passed us and the angry swells returned to our accustomed rolling waves, we began to assess the damage. All of the front windows were gone, broken glass was everywhere. As we cleaned up, we kept finding bits and pieces of glass all the way back to the bunk room. The cabin doors were ripped off. The galley was a disaster area, pots and pans were scattered all about. Everything was saturated and soaked with sea water.

"The outside of the boat was just as bad. Ropes, the ones that still remained were sprawled over the back deck like a den of uncoiled snakes, mangled and tangled. The trawling doors were dangling and swaying over the sides. The right side outrigger was bent back like a half-opened jack knife. The outrigger on the left was half submerged in the water bobbing up and down with the ebb and flow of the wake. The main mast was slightly bowed. We picked up the ruined riggers, re-coiled the ropes and hung them back up.

"And so, we came sputtering back to home Port crippled, licking our wounds. After we got off the boat and went home to our families, we told them what happened and how scared we were. We didn't know how we survived. Our mother Isidra saw the fright still consuming us. She took us to Dona Maria, a local faith healer. Dona Maria welcomed us with her always saintly hospitality. She listened attentively to our tribulation and near-death ordeal. She sat us down on two wooden chairs next to her dining table and asked us to wait.

"She asked our mother and wives to follow her outside. They sat on some benches under a large ancient mesquite tree that shaded her small front yard.

"She then proceeded to her herb garden. Dona Maria was an old lady. She had been old as far back as we could remember. We had known her all our lives and she had always been old. She wore the same woolen grey shawl over a grey-and-white-pleated ankle-long dress, day in and day out. A rose apron of yellow, red, and pink flowers had two pockets sown on the front. In the left pocket, she kept a man's black and grey checkered handkerchief, that she pulled out occasionally to wipe her old wrinkled hands and lips. In her right pocket she kept several small bundles of fragrant herbs tied with cotton twine. There she stored wads of efflorescent herb clusters.

"She shuffled to her herbs. She kept them behind a rickety wooden gate and waist-high fence on the front right side of her property. As she entered her garden, she crossed herself and began to pray in a low lisping whisper.

"She cautiously snapped off several basil stems. The ones with blossoms, and a few other herbal branches. She came back inside the house without saying a word to us. She shuffled back past her two patients to her kerosene burning stove. She took an earthen clay pitcher that she filled with rain water she collected in a cistern in her back yard. She stripped the blooms off the basil and sprinkled them in the rain water and adjusted the burner flame to a simmering violet hue.

"She returned to us and instructed us to lay prone on the floor of her small living room. She went to an adjacent room and returned with two white sheets. She spread the sheets over us, covering us from the neck down to our feet. She went back to her stove, turned off the burner, took the clay pot with rain water and the basil flowers and poured it into a large wooden bowl. She placed the bowl between us. She then went to an altar she had decorated with aromatic red, yellow and pink roses and green, red and white ribbons, in the left corner of her living room next to the front windows, opposite the door to the right.

"The shrine had a picture of Jesus with his Sacred Heart exposed. A small statue of Our Lady of Guadalupe stood to His right, a statue of Our Lady of San Juan to his left side. Each had a pink rosary around her neck. Right below them were seven lit church candles illuminating the shrine. In-between each was a freshly cut, short-stemmed red rose in a small glass with water. Both the Virgin of Guadalupe and Virgin of San Juan love roses. Three drinking glasses filled with water were on the top shelf, one directly in front of each statue. Water for them to drink.

"We watched as she crossed herself, prayed the Our Father and two Hail Marys. Afterwards, she stood in silent meditation for a few seconds. She took a small bottle of holy water she kept on the shrine, turned and approached us. In a low whisper she asked us to close our eyes, take three deep breaths and relax.

"She told us everything was going to be okay. She asked us if we knew how to pray the rosary. We replied that we did. She told us to start with the Our Father, and continue praying the five Glorious Mysteries, silently to ourselves, until she asked to stop. With eyes closed we did as we were told.

"She lit some herbal, stemmed incense and placed it on a stone slab she had placed on the floor a few inches above our heads. As the mild fragrant vapors rose, she whispered her petitions. She poured holy water into the wooden bowl with rain water and basil blossoms. She dipped her basil stems in the water mixture and sprinkled us with wet refreshing drops. She then took some more water into her cupped hand, rubbed and stroked our heads. She took her herbal Buena, and ran it over our sheet-covered bodies, lightly brushing us back and forth from head to toe.

"After this, she took the burning incense, cleansing us with it from head to toe, praying all the while. After she had sprinkled us with holy water, swept us with the herbs and cleansed us with the incense, she told us to stop praying. She removed the white sheets from our bodies, folded them and placed them to one side. She asked us to stand and follow her outside to where our mother and wives were waiting under the mesquite tree. She told all of us in a low voice that everything was okay now. We should go home and go to bed until the morning. But before going to bed, we needed to drink a cup of warm tea from some yerba Buena (mint) leaves she gave us.

"We did as she said. The next day we woke up rested and refreshed. We weren't frightened anymore. The fright of our lives had been expelled. We had a big hearty breakfast of eggs, mashed pinto beans, fried potatoes, orange slices and creamed coffee. We went back to the boat and began to repair it for our next fishing trip."

They fished through a couple of hurricanes, one off the coast of Mexico. Billy and about thirty other boats had to pay the Mexican Government a fee government for safe harbor. During Hurricane Cindy, he went in to Lake Charles, Louisiana, to ride out the storm.

One time when they were short-handed, Billy had to help head shrimp on the back deck. He squeezed as many heads off as fast as he could for a few minutes, then dashed to the wheelhouse to steer the boat clear of any danger ahead. During one of those sit-ins on the back deck, he lost track of time and the boat rammed into another boat. Thankfully, no one on board either boat was injured.

Billy was raised Catholic, but shrimping is not a go-to-Sunday-Mass lifestyle. He attended the Mass and Blessing of the Fleet celebrated every year at the beginning of the season. His faith however inspired him always have religious pictures of Christ on the cross and the Virgin Mary aboard the boat for safe voyages.

17

NOE LOPEZ

In our family, it's always been about the water.

NOE'S GRANDFATHER AND FATHER harvested oysters and set trot lines in the Lower Laguna Madre for many years. His grandfather, Thomas Reyes, owned a sailboat which he used for his fishing operation and also worked as a fishing guide. Born in 1923, Thomas would become Port Isabel's chief of police after World

War II. During that time, he was the town's only lawman, besides the county constables. In addition to his
lawman's job and his fishing guide services, he opened
and operated Reyes Bakery, a landmark business that
is still in operation today. He also owned a few cantinas and an oyster house. He became one of the town's
major employers.

When Noe entered the world in 1958, Port Isabel
was prospering from a growing shrimping industry. Like
his brothers, he was taken out on the bay almost before
he could walk. His dad took him fishing commercially
as a helper when he was eight. At nine, he began working for his grandfather in the bakery. When he turned
twelve, he was back fishing in the bay. The grandkids
preferred to find work outside the bakery because they
didn't get paid for working for their grandfather. They
were allowed to eat as much sweet bread as they wanted, but two pieces of his delicious Mexican sweet bread
was all it took to fill their small bellies. Plus, they had
to sweep, mop, wash pots and pans, run errands and
any other chores their grandfather ordered them to do.

After high school, Noe's dad wanted him to go to
college. When he refused, his dad said "Fine. In that
case, go find and make your way in the world because
I'm not going to support you anymore. I've done my
part." Noe walked the docks looking for work. With his
ever present bravado and outgoing personality (which
he still carries with him), he talked a good game and
landed a job.

His first job was on the *Debbie G*, a wooden-hulled
boat, He started with less than a promising beginning.
Noe spent eighteen days at sea, sick the entire time. Although he may have doubted it at the time, he survived

and would never suffer from seasickness again. Henry, the owner, must have seen promise in his new header. Within a few months, he offered to teach him to be a captain. He told Noe to shadow him; that he had to learn from the bottom up. From that day on, Noe stayed on watch with Henry and soaked up every bit of information Henry provided.

Once after Noe took down the rigging, Henry took it apart. He told Noe, "Now put it back together." He needed to understand the importance of each piece.

Shortly after Noe turned eighteen, Henry told him to "grab his rags (gear)." Fear gripped Noe. Was Henry firing him? When he failed to move, Henry repeated the order. He pointed to a bigger and newer boat. "You wanted to be a captain. There's your boat."

While Noe struggled with apprehension, Henry instructed him to find an experienced rig man and everything would be fine. "Just remember, take it slow, one day at a time."

His brother Joe had been shrimping for fifteen years. Noe asked him to join him as a rig man on his new boat, the steel-hulled *Andy G.*

Joe agreed to be his little brother's rig man and off they went. A brand new boat with a brand new captain at the helm and an experienced rig man, off to make a name for himself.

Noe first fished the shallow waters off the beach of South Padre Island where the shrimp, both brown and white, were small (60-to-80 count to make a pound). It took hours of back-breaking work to produce enough pounds to make a living. The price paid for small-sized shrimp is much lower. Everyone had to work longer and harder, but it was all that he knew when he began.

After he had been a captain for a year or more, he answered a call that changed his fishing career. A man had been issuing a distress call for several days but no one answered him. Noe remembered that the man radioing for help sounded like a black man. He didn't know if that was why his call had been ignored or if he was the only one who heard him. When he answered the call and came up alongside the boat, the man (Jimmy) asked for the captain. "'I'm it," Noe answered. Jimmy found it hard to believe that someone as young as Noe could be the captain.

Jimmy's boat was dead in the water. Noe had never towed another disabled boat into port before. He had to call on another boat for help. Once they reached Port Aransas, a strong norther blew in and they had to stay the night.

Jimmy had twelve-hundred pounds of jumbo shrimp on his boat. When Noe refused to take any money for helping him, Jimmy offered to teach him how to fish for the big shrimp. For the next thirty days, Noe followed Jimmy, charting and memorizing the hot spots for the "big ones." At the end of the thirty days, they said goodbye and parted ways. Noe spent the rest of his shrimping career working the deep waters chasing and bringing in the "Big ones." He considered it working smart instead of working hard. He worked smart because he had a good teacher and he was a willing student.

A couple of years later. Noe had to go into Port Aransas for minor repairs. He saw Jimmy's boat tied to the dock. He went over to say hello to his friend. When he got to the boat, he asked a man that was on the boat if Captain Jimmy was still the skipper.

The man answered back that he was the skipper of the boat. Noe asked if he knew the previous captain named Jimmy. The man said he didn't know Jimmy. He said it was his boat. He had the boat built for him and that he was the only captain the boat had ever had.

To this day, Noe can't figure out what happened to his ghost captain, Jimmy.

Over his nineteen-year shrimping career, Noe worked with three rig men and four headers. He believed that if you found good men and paid them well, they would stay with you and they did. He believed in having good discipline and leading by example. He was firm but fair and his crew respected that. He never allowed drinking on his boat.

Over the years, he worked for Bill Zimmerman, Walter Zimmerman, Sammy Snodgrass, the Tower family and Andreas Garza. Most gave him strong support. They provided excellent boats in mint working condition and enough bonus pay incentives at the end of the year to keep him working at his top performance level. Noe admired Andreas especially. Andreas came over from Mexico as an immigrant with zero money in his pockets. He got a job on a shrimp boat, saved his money and eventually became a millionaire with a small fleet of four boats and real estate property.

"Bill Zimmerman would always tell me I was his number one captain," Noe said, "but it didn't take me long to figure out that he said that to every one of his captains when they came back in with the boats' bins filled with shrimp. It worked. He had business smarts. But, if you were not producing to his high standard and expectations, he had no problem letting you know you were slacking." There was always a lot of pressure from boat owners to bring in big cargo loads of shrimp. Peer pressure is prevalent among fleet company crews. The younger captains, anxious to prove themselves, are especially competitive. Their higher productivity puts pressure on the older more experienced captains who do not want to be outproduced and outperformed by the young "whippersnappers."

Life was good, the money was good—but as we all know, "life is not always a bowl of cherries." Noe still remembers the day that Sammy Snodgrass fired him. Sammy had given him a new boat to captain, the *Southern Cross*. He transferred all his belongings from his old boat, the *War Wagon*. Later, he received a call from Sammy, who accused him of leaving a bag of marijuana under his bed. Sammy fired him. When Noe later proved to him that the weed belonged to *War Wagon*'s new captain, Sammy apologized and offered him his job back. Disappointed and hurt by Sammy's lack of trust after all the years he fished for him, Noe left in anger. He never worked for Sammy again.

When the government introduced TED regulations, the threat of fines became a reality. If a shrimper was caught closing the device, he could receive a $25,000 fine and up to thirty years in prison. Noe felt that shrimpers were being wrongly blamed for the decline of the sea turtle population. But the law is the law and you have to abide by it or pay the consequences. All shrimpers knew that the introduction of the TEDs to their fishing nets was going to cost them part of their catch. They just didn't know how much. The government hired scientists and marine biologists that conducted the studies of the TEDs' efficiency on shrimp boats, reporting that shrimpers would lose three to ten percent of their shrimp. Noe had to find out for himself. He was going to conduct his own tests. He took the chance. One night fishing off the Louisiana coast, he dragged for nine hours. On one side of the boat, he had the TED on his nets working. On the other side of the boat he had the TED closed/disabled. He found a 40% difference between the two sides. For every one hundred pounds of shrimp caught with the nets that had the TED closed, he found the nets that had the TED working had forty pounds less. He conducted his experiment again and again. All of his drags gave him similar results.

Later, when the TEDs had been modified, the catch loss decreased significantly. Perhaps the U.S. Department of Fisheries should have consulted with veteran shrimping captains like Noe Lopez before going out on their own to do field lab work.

18

REY LOPEZ

A rig man must constantly be alert to weather and the sea.

REY LOPEZ IS NOE'S older brother. Like his father and grandfather before him, he grew up on the water. He doesn't remember a time he didn't fish.

He worked in the shrimping industry as a boy and for about fifteen years as a young man. Beginning as a header, he soon became a rig man.

He never wanted the responsibility of a captain but he loved performing many of the captain's duties. He especially enjoyed taking watch at night while the captain slept.

Rey was responsible for keeping the equipment in good working order. This included the nets, the rigging and the winch.

After years at sea he grew tired of the long fishing trips. Today's shrimp boats are all equipped with freezers on board. This allows them to extend their fishing days from ten to fifteen days when shrimpers fished on ice boats to a minimum of thirty days, all the way up to twice that of sixty days.

Because of this, Rey decided to return to commercial bay fishing on his own. He now takes his eighteen-foot outboard motor boat out in the morning, sets and baits his trot lines and comes back before supper time. Early the next morning, he returns to check his lines. He unhooks all regulation-size black drum and puts them in his boat, re-baits the hook and moves on to the next hook until he reaches the end of the line.

Hooks and bait do not discriminate against which fish they snatch. Commercial bay fisherman routinely find red fish and trout hooked on their line. By law they are required to unhook and release them. Red fish and trout are listed as game fish by the State of Texas, and may only be fished for, with a sports fishing state-issued license. Today because of state fish regulations, he only fishes for black drum, which he sells locally to make a living. The current law is that commercial bay fishermen can only set their lines from Monday morning to Friday noon.

Sports fisherman are allowed to fish seven days a week, twenty-four hours a day. They may fish for the state-listed game fish as well as for black drum. The present state fishing laws have almost wiped out the commercial fishermen in Texas. Rey is one of no more than a handful (maybe five at the most), commercial fisherman who fish for black drum in Port Isabel. If the state of Texas would regulate black drum, and keep it only for commercial fisherman, they would be able to make a better living fishing. But such is not the case.

19

JOSE MARTINEZ

I like being on the water and I like the work.

LIKE MOST OF THE boys his age in Port Isabel, Jose grew up with shrimping. His dad was a shrimper and once he was old enough, Jose spent summers on a boat. Although he has six brothers and four sisters, he is the only sibling who became a shrimper.

After high school, his mother and some of his siblings moved to Baytown, Texas. He went with them. This was during the early seventies and work in the Baytown / Houston area was plentiful, especially in the oil refineries. He found work there and stayed for a while. But eventually the sea called him, and he returned to Port Isabel. He had experience working as a header and it didn't take him long to get hired on a boat. He never moved away again.

He travels to Baytown to visit his mother after the end of every shrimp season. He freezes as much shrimp and fish as he can during the season. When he goes to Baytown, he arrives with loads of shrimp and fish for his mother and siblings. They celebrate his return by having a grand traditional Port Isabel-style shrimp and fish fry, with plenty of beer to drink and music to dance to. His mother is the happiest one at the fry fest. She has her seaman son back with her. He has survived another year at sea.

Jose has spent more than twenty years working as a header on shrimp boats.

"I like my work and I wouldn't want to do anything else." His face lights up when he talks about his life on a boat. "I love the sea and I miss it when I'm not out there."

With only three crew members most of the season, each holds a necessary and unique place in the shrimping process. Although the primary duty of a header is to head the shrimp, he is also responsible for keeping the boat clean, helping with the winch, checking and cleaning the nets daily, inspecting, coiling and hanging all the ropes and lines, assisting with minor repairs, cleaning up the kitchen and galley after meals as well helping raise and lower the nets into the water.

Jose takes pride in his skills. He can head a seventy-pound basket of shrimp in about an hour. He can hold seven or eight in his hand at a time (depending on size), using both hands. After heading the shrimp, he washes and packs them in the crates, each holding one-hundred pounds. He helps the rig man lower them down to the hull bins for freezing. Captains and rig men appreciate and value experienced headers. The captain, with input from the rig man, hires the header and will pay top dollar for them. His salary is paid out of the captain's and rig man's share of the profits and is calculated per one-hundred pound boxes of shrimp.

On a typical trip, about forty days at sea, they lower the nets into the water before sunset and pick them up about 1:00 am. After the nets are hauled in and emptied on the deck, the nets are dropped again. The header then puts on his rubber gloves, places his bushel baskets next to where he is going to sit, sits down on his low stool close to the deck, grabs his small, short hoe-like shovel, hoes some shrimp towards him between his legs and begins to squeeze the heads off the shrimp with speed and precision.

As he fills one bushel basket all the way to the top, he pushes it to one side, grabs another basket, places it next to him, and continues to dig into the shrimp mound, hoeing more shrimp between his legs and starts working on filling the next basket. This process is repeated until the last shrimp is headed.

The rig man is doing the same thing on the opposite side of the pile of shrimp. With each basket that is filled, the mound gets smaller. The header and rig man move closer and closer to the center of the pile, until they virtually come face to face with each other. A lot of the time, headers and rig men will take a few seconds to stand up, stretch their back, light a cigarette, and put it between their lips where it will dangle until the tobacco burns close to the filter. They will then take the stub from between their lips, flip to one side and continue their heading without missing a beat.

After the last shrimp is headed, they hose down and wash the basket's contents removing as much Gulf bottom mud off the shrimp as possible, dip the shrimp in a solution to keep them fresh frozen and lower them down into the freezer.

The header will then hose, wash and scrape the deck clean and prepare it for the next net pickup. Depending on how many shrimp they are catching the process from start to finish will take four to five hours. The last net drag will be picked up at dawn or at sunrise. After the last drag of the night is finished, all the shrimp is packed away in the freezer, the deck is washed clean, the nets hung and secured. They sit down for a big hearty breakfast. The crew has two big meals a day—breakfast and dinner with some snacks in between.

"We eat really well." Jose spoke about breakfasts of eggs, bacon, tortillas, biscuits, fruit and a soda. Dinners might be steaks, chicken, fish or shrimp. The rig man prepares the meals and most have a reputation as being good cooks.

By noon, he has finished cleaning up and is ready to catch four or five hours sleep. Then it's time to wake up and ready the nets for the next night's trawl.

The more shrimp, the better the pay for the crew and the boat owner. After the big nets are in the water, the smaller try net (a smaller net to gauge shrimp numbers) is also lowered. It is checked every thirty minutes or so to keep count. It's also used to determine if they are dragging a good area where shrimp are plentiful. If not, the captain will then set another course in search of a better fishing spot.

When the boat is anchored and they're not sleeping, crew members like to take leisure time for deep sea fishing. Jose loves ling but they also catch red snapper and other species. Squid is the bait of choice. When the boat returns home, each crew member is allowed by law to keep two ling and four red snappers. Other fish are not restricted.

Shrimpers must have a license to fish. The license is renewed every year at a current cost of fifty dollars.

Over the years, Jose has worked on ten different boats. For the past ten years, his work has mainly been for Captain Jesse Delgado, on the *Miss Joanna*. In a typical year, he will make seven trips—each lasting about forty days.

Headers make a modest living and they work hard for their money. They do not however share in paying for any of the crew's expenses. Their only expenses are the cigarettes they smoke, their work clothes and their sea boots. In the process of bringing shrimp to American consumers, they are worth their weight in gold. If the shrimp is not headed within a certain amount of time, they are not good to eat.

"I like to drink a beer and see my friends when I get home." Back on land about a week at a time, he enjoys socializing. Jose is a contented man at sixty-three years of age, living the life he loves, and working at the job he loves.

A header's tools

20

MARES MARTINEZ

They were the best days of my life. I loved shrimping.

AS A YOUNG BOY, Mares and his dad would row to South Bay to harvest oysters. South Bay is a small inlet south of the Brownsville Ship Channel about half a mile once you pass the Brazos de Santiago Pass and enter the Laguna Madre. Because the Laguna Madre is a hyper-saline bay, locals arguably say its oysters are the best tasting you can find. Mares rowed their small boat from Port Isabel to South Bay. The trip is between one or two miles depending on where you leave Port Isabel. They gathered oysters all day, five to six bushels total. Because of the heavy load, his dad would raise the small canvas sail and head for home. Once back on land they would tote the bushels to their house, where the next phase and perhaps the best part of oyster harvesting began, the shucking of the oysters. The best part is the eating of fresh oysters right off the shell. The watery, milky and surprisingly sweet oysters were a special treat for the family.

He and his siblings would savory slurp a few before taking some into the kitchen to their mother. As she breaded them in corn meal and fried them in the big black cast iron skillet, Mom would briskly spread out perfectly round kneaded flour tortillas and lay them flat on the piping comal. By the time the oysters were cooked, she would have a six-to-eight high stack of steaming-hot aromatic tortillas wrapped in a cotton cloth.

Mares recalled the French-fried potatoes and mashed refried beans that completed the meal. During the preparation of supper, Mares and his dad feverishly shucked as many oysters as they could. After supper, they would return to the oysters and continue shucking until the job was done and they retired to bed. The next day, they would get up early and can them into gallon-sized metal containers. They would then go to their regular restaurant customers. They sold them for one dollar a gallon. Once the oysters were sold, they repeated the process all over again.

His dad started shrimping and spent nine years aboard the *Wild Duck*. In 1945–1946, when the Ports of Harlingen and Mansfield started dredging, he went to work for them. The dredging sadly killed many of the oyster beds in the Lower Laguna Madre. The bountiful beds were indiscriminately covered with mud and soot by the dredge spoils. The environmental damage to oysters was tremendous. To this day commercial oyster harvesting in the Lower Laguna Madre is limited to one or two fishermen who still go out to gather oysters for personal consumption and to sell a few gallons to friends whenever they can. There are no more local oysters to be had.

One of nine boys, Mares grew up poor. After third grade, his dad pulled him out of school to help support the family. Always aware of his lack of education, he encouraged his own children to study hard and choose a life other than shrimping.

By the age of twenty, Mares was a captain. He was the skipper of the *Carlet Ann* and fished for Wallace Boudreaux. Mares worked for Samuel Snodgrass in the 1960s. During the summer he fished up and down the Texas coast and some in Louisiana. As the shrimp migrated south to Mexican waters during the cold winter months, so did he. He fished the Mexican coast all the way down to the Bay of Campeche. He loved and has many fond memories of the years he fished in Campeche, especially the money he earned.

In September 1967, Hurricane Beulah came ashore directly on top of Port Isabel. She brought with her one-hundred-thirty-five mile-an-hour winds and countless tornadoes. These powerful winds inflicted tremendous damage to Port Isabel and its shrimping fleet. Mares's boat was spared the wrath of Beulah. It just so happened that he was on his way to St. Augustine, Florida when Beulah smashed Port Isabel.

After fishing for many years as a captain, he came home from one of his fishing trips. As he and his wife Josefina, affectionately known as Chepa, were talking about their future in the shrimping industry, he mentioned to her that his dream was to own and operate his own shrimp boat. He gleefully recalls Chepa asking him. "Well, Mares, what is it that you need to buy a boat of your own?"

"I need money," he answered.

"How much money do you need?"

"Lots of money," he replied.

She took him to their bedroom.

"Lift the mattress," she said.

He did as she asked.

After he'd lifted and pushed the mattress of their bed to one side, Chepa gathered several stacks of un-cashed payroll checks laid out on top of the box spring mattress—and handed the checks over to him.

As he took the checks, he asked for an explanation.

"Well, every time you returned from shrimping and gave me money to pay the bills, buy groceries, and get the kids what they needed, I saved the rest under the mattress."

It has always been common practice for shrimpers coming in from a successful fishing trip to take a few boxes of shrimp for themselves. They sell them to local restaurants or to small seafood markets. Then they divide the money among themselves to have some cash in their pockets until the big cargo is weighed, processed and paid.

Of course, boat owners don't like it. They know it happens—but as long as the unspoken practice is not abused, they cringe and look the other way. Somehow they feel that if they don't see what happens, it won't hurt as much. They figure that as long as they are making good money, they will bear the loss.

Perhaps Mares gave Chepa some of that money and that is how she managed the household expenses and saved the uncashed checks.

"Take the checks, cash them and buy your boat," she told him. Mares did just that and became a boat owner. He sold this first boat several years later for $80,000 and bought his pride and joy, the *Magic Valley*, a sixty-two-foot wooden boat, which he owned for ten years. A few years after that he bought the *Miss Bernillia*, a sixty-two-foot, steel-hulled boat from William Zimmerman for $125,000.

"Wooden boats need a lot of care and maintenance. You have to dry dock them every six months. They get a lot of termites, and if you don't scrape and exterminate them, the pests will eat you out of your boat," he explained.

Mares recalled catching a huge turtle once. It tore up the net and was too heavy for the winch. That happened before the government issued the TED regulations. Like all shrimpers, he didn't like the regulations because he didn't see a problem. Now that regulation and a thousand-plus others are part and parcel of shrimping life.

Mares recalled several squalls with waves around twenty-feet high. "You can't run against them," he said.

Different times while fishing in Florida, he was caught on the edge of several hurricanes. Outrunning one, he made it to Freeport, Texas. He vividly remembers the jetties being covered by angry breaker foam. He was familiar with the Freeport jetties, having navigated them many times before. Knowing where he was at all times enabled him to steer his boat in safely.

One of Mares's fondest memories of his younger days was making friends and hanging out with singer Freddy Fender. Back then Freddy Fender had not yet adopted his stage name. He was Baldemar Huerta. "We had lots of good times. We'd go to a bar and drink. When the money ran out, Freddy would bring out his guitar and sing. The other customers sent us rounds of beers as long as Freddy continued singing. He performed all over the Valley on both sides of the border. We had a really good time. It ended when he got drafted."

Mares has witnessed his share of injuries, some minor and some major—and he has lost friends to the sea. A couple guys he knew fell overboard. Fortunately, in both cases, they were rescued. Both Mares and Billy Holland spoke memorably of Juan Castillo, a good friend and fishing buddy. Juan accidentally fell overboard one night and the Gulf of Mexico claimed his body forever. However, his spirit lives in his surviving children—and the Port Isabel community still remembers him and his fate.

Mares loved the sea. He still holds a place for her in his heart. They shared many days and nights together. She produced a bounty that enabled him to have a good life. For this he will always be grateful. He was able to raise his family and live well. He understood and respected her many moods—sometimes tranquil, calm and gentle and other times aroused, rough and mad.

Over the years, he enjoyed the camaraderie with his peers. He made many friends and always felt that they held a kind of fraternal brotherhood bond. He cherishes the quiet pleasant times and celebrates overcoming the many challenging times. But what he loved most of all, and always looked forward to, was his homecoming. He loved seeing the happy faces of his wife and children as they sat together at their favorite restaurant, Vermillion, in Brownsville. The owners had to put several tables together in order to accommodate the eleven family members. Everyone was dressed in their finest and over the years, dining at Vermillion's became a favorite tradition.

For forty-five years, Mares fished the Gulf of Mexico from Port Isabel Texas, the entire length of the Texas coast, Louisiana, Mississippi, Alabama, the Florida coast all the way down to the Keys. He fished Mexico from Tuxpan, Tampico and all the way down to Campeche.

Later on during his shrimping years, Mares contributed his energy, time and vast experience of commercial fishing to public service. He is a past board member of the Texas Shrimpers Association and served as an elected board member on the Port Isabel/San Benito Navigation District for four years.

Mares was eighteen when he married his seventeen year-old-sweetheart, Chepa. They raised nine children—five girls and four boys. After sixty-two years of marriage, he lost Chepa, the love of his life, to Alzheimer's.

21

DON JESUS ROSALES

Rig Man

DON JESUS CAME FROM Mexico when he was a young man. He got a job on the docks unloading shrimp boats. He soon learned that shrimpers earned more money than dock workers. He got a job as a header. A few years later, he learned the skills and trade of a rig man. He worked as a rig man for thirty-plus years before retiring.

When asked if he ever captained a boat, Don Jesus said no. He never had any desire to become a captain.

He was happy rigging. "I was never any good at giving orders. Being a captain is too much responsibility, everything that happens on the boat, good or bad, weighs on his shoulders. I never wanted to deal with that."

He preferred to get on board when it was time to go out on a trip, get the nets and rigging ready, set sail and fish. Don Jesus feels it takes a special person to be a rig man.

The most important part of being a good rig man is to learn how your captain operates and how he likes things done on the boat. "You have to study his moods. You have to know when to talk to him and when to leave him alone. You have to learn how he likes his meals cooked, his coffee brewed, and how to ration the groceries in accordance to the number of days you are going to stay out."

One of the things a rig man does not want to tell the captain, is that they have run out of food and need to go in to port, especially if they are catching shrimp. A rig man has to anticipate a captain's every move. He has to know the captain as well as the captain knows himself. The rig man is the captain's first mate and often times his conscience. "Many times we are the go-between from the crew to the captain. Kind of like the wife is the go-between from the children to the father."

The rig man will always keep the captain informed of the crew's wishes, conversations, discussions and complaints. Before the rig man goes to the captain to let him know what the crew is talking about and wants, he first will talk it over, resolve and settle the problem with the crew. He will listen to their grievances and decide how to handle the situation. He knows exactly how the captain will react and what his answer will be to requests or complaints. The rig man will tell the crew what needs to be done and work out the issue with the crew without having to go to the captain. The captain expects this from his rig man. However, the rig man still has to tell the captain what happened and how he handled the situation. Most of the time, the captain is satisfied how the rig man took care of a problem—however, he will still talk to the crew about decisions he made. This usually takes place during the evening meal. The captain has the final word and after that, there is no more discussion on the matter.

Yes, rig man are special fishermen. They are the ones who make the marriage of captain and rig man out at sea work. Without a good rig man on board, chances are the fishing trip will end in disaster.

22

LINDA AND RED SAGNES

Port Isabel gained national attention when Dan Rather came
to town after Hurricane Beulah.
Linda Sagnes

*

Shrimping was a rough life and there are many stories to tell.
Red Sagnes

EVERETT "RED" SAGNES GREW up in Minnesota and
first visited Port Isabel when he served in the U.S.

Navy. He met and married Linda Perez, a daughter of a local pioneer family, and took her to Minnesota. They returned to Port Isabel in 1960—and have lived there ever since. The house they live in was originally one of two built before Derry Elementary School (the original Port Isabel High School) opened.

Linda grew up in Port Isabel and remembers the influx of the big boats from Louisiana. She was still at the Catholic grade school when the Louisianans came. They mostly settled around the Garriga area, in the same neighborhood where she lived. Predominately Catholic, many parents enrolled their children in the school.

She remembers Mayor Charles "B. B." Burnell, the shrimp fiestas, and a time when girls were not allowed around the docks. Like most Port Isabel children, she grew up bilingual and bicultural. If you were Mexican-American and Catholic, the odds were that you were educated at Our Lady Star of the Sea Catholic School. Mexican-American mothers and grandmothers were devout Catholics. Priests and nuns held revered positions in the community. Family life was centered around Mom, Dad, grandparents, aunts, uncles, cousins, neighbors, the church, the Catholic school and its catechism.

Red's first job was for E.W. Cateora, owner and operator of Brazos Fish House. When he started, he earned thirty-seven dollars per week. E.W. was known as a short-tempered man. Because of this characteristic, he acquired the nick-name on the docks as "la rabia." In Spanish "rabia" means rabies.

"I walked in, he gave me a big box of bills and a checkbook," Red remembered. He worked as the bookkeeper for nearly a year before he secured a position at Twin City Co-op. Within six months, he became the manager. Twin City, a cooperative of many shrimpers, exposed him to all facets of the industry and its people. When he started, there were only wooden-hulled, ice boats.

Port Isabel grew by leaps and bounds once the Louisianans arrived. Big boats replaced small fishing boats, numerous fish houses and consequently many support businesses opened as a result. Twin City Co-op became one of the biggest shrimp processors in town, shipping most of their product to Philadelphia. At that time, the shrimpers brought the shrimp in with the heads on.

"In the beginning we were weighing the heads. When a boat docked, a worker from the fish house drove around town honking his horn. Housewives clamored for the heading jobs because they knew there was money to be earned. This extra income contributed towards buying school clothes and supplies for their children. During the summer, most of the children worked as well," Linda recalled. The mothers brought the children with them because there was no one left to watch them. Everyone was at the fish houses heading shrimp. The children helped as much and as long as they could. Whatever little they contributed towards the total weight at the end of the day earned them enough money to go to the local movie on Sunday afternoon after Mass and the family dinner.

Although both recalled that drinking on the docks when a boat came in was a way of life, Linda remembers that the men were always gracious and respectful whenever wives and kids were around. "I never saw any public drunkenness."

Shrimpers drank their beer while working on the boats. After work, they went home. They then took their family out for a fine supper and a good time at one of the local restaurants. Sometimes dads took the family to Matamoros, Mexico for an even finer dining experience. Port Isabel shrimping families prided themselves in patronizing fine dining establishments in Matamoros, like the Texas Bar, The U.S. Bar and El Senioral. The women dressed in their finest, the girls wore patent leather shoes and ribbons in their hair and the boys all had a short haircut, starched shirt and pants, and shined shoes. Mom and Dad enjoyed a few cocktails, dined on steak and quail, and danced to orchestra music. The kids loved the fresh-squeezed lemonade. Matamoros businesses loved the shrimpers. They had money and they spent it. The economy on both sides of the border was booming. Going back and forth was a common practice.

Over the years, Red and Linda owned six boats, though no more than three at a time. Today, pictures of each boat line their kitchen wall.

"Shrimping was often a rough life and owners found themselves at the mercy of thieving captains," Red said. Once a captain on the *Extreme*, the Sagnes' first boat, took it to Port Arthur where he unloaded and sold the shrimp, keeping the money. Although Red recovered the boat, the captain was never again seen around Port Isabel.

Another time, the captain of the *WG Junior*, took the boat to Louisiana where he sold the shrimp and kept the money.

Most of the owners have their Mexico stories and Red is no exception. The Mexican Coast Guard seized the *Señorita Nancy* and took it to Tampico. They let the crew remain on board, which was not the norm. Red and Linda went to Tampico and paid a $15,000 fine. The Mexicans didn't appreciate seeing a woman on a shrimp boat. When the Sagnes' said she was one of the owners, they had no choice but to allow her on the docks to check on her crew. Linda brought the crew food, personal hygiene products and messages from home. She had grown up with the crew and before leaving Port Isabel, had visited with their families, promising she and Red would do everything they could to bring the men home safe and sound.

The *Extreme*

The *Lady Robin*

The *Señora Linda*

23

SAMMY SNODGRASS

Shrimping's been good to me.

SAMMY, A THIRD-GENERATION SHRIMPER in the Port Isabel/Brownsville area, owns S&S Sales in the Brownsville Shrimp Basin. He's proud that his son, Jack, is carrying on the family tradition and now works with him. He hopes that shrimping continues to be as good for his son and descendants as it has been for his father, his brother and him.

In 1865, his grandfather, like most Virginians, lost everything in the Civil War. Battles had been fought on his land and there was nothing left. Needing work, he went down to Chesapeake Bay where he worked as a fisherman. When the railroad came through during Reconstruction, he traveled to Georgia and again worked on a fishing boat. He eventually owned and operated several small boats at the time of his death in 1929.

Sammy's dad, then in his early teens, took over running one of the boats for his grandmother. She lost the other boats but he secured a couple more boats by the time he was drafted in World War II.

When Sammy's dad returned, he started again with one boat. He did well enough to save some money. In 1947, shrimping friends in Texas urged him to join them. He came to Port Isabel and went to work managing the heading house at Magic Valley Processing. Over the next few years, he continued to save money, built a successful business and purchased several boats.

During their late teens, Sammy and his brother got in trouble for shooting ducks. As punishment, his dad put them to work on a boat. A couple of years later, Sammy's dad sold all of his boats to a South American company. Following the only job he knew, he moved the family there and fished for three years, from 1962–1965. By the time he tired of living abroad, he brought his family and three boats back to Port Isabel. They settled and lived in Brownsville, but he docked his boats in Port Isabel.

Sammy went to college. After graduation, he returned to the family business. They fished the entire Gulf from Florida and Louisiana to Mexico and the Bay of Campeche. During these years, U.S. and Mexican boats fished along each other's coasts with no questions asked. Shrimp were plentiful and business was booming.

In 1976, the U.S. Government decided to become more involved in the fishing industry. They formed several marine preservation committees and issued multi-million dollar grants to coastal universities, state and U.S. fishery agencies to conduct scientific studies on the preservation of the fishing industry.

The universities hired all kinds of Marine biologists and interns, and bought shrimp boats. They set up those shrimp boats as working labs at sea for future marine biologist. They also set up labs on land to analyze and interpret the results. Coincidently and consequently, to make it appear inclusive, they budgeted a small amount of money to contract some shrimpers as consultants.

All of a sudden, millions of federal dollars went into the study of shrimping in the United States. A whole new cash cow was created. Years later and millions and millions of taxpayer dollars later, they came up with the U.S.-defined 200-mile economic zone. Mexico followed suit. Keep in mind that the U.S. officials were sharing some data of their studies with Mexican fishing officials. As a result, and through back door channel negotiations, Mexico agreed to a deal, allowing U.S. fisherman to fish Mexican waters over the next four years. You never deal with Mexican officials and get a deal worked out without the principals getting their significant cut.

In the 1980s, when the Navigation Channel refused to renew his lease, Sammy moved his operation to the Brownsville Navigation Shrimp Basin. He built a fleet of eight boats.

He sold one and in 2010, he lost one to a fire. The boat, in Louisiana, burned for forty-two hours and is still stuck there in layers of mud.

"We have to fish year round for the crew to make a living," Sammy said. "Over the years, my crews have mostly been good by shrimping crew standards. Once in awhile, we'll have a crew member who gets too rowdy and ends up getting in trouble. But when you are dealing with seafaring fishermen, you know to expect that sooner, rather than later, you will get a radio call from one of your captains saying that someone in your crew had one too many beers in a distant port and that requires your intervention. It comes with the territory when dealing with hard-working, hard-drinking shrimpers. They live day to day. When they are out at sea, there is usually no problem. They work hard day and night. But once they come into a port, they hit the bars and anything can happen.

"Every time a boat has to go into port away from home, we tell our captains to first analyze the situation. If they can make it back to home port, then by all means come in. If the boat is unable to make it back, go into the nearest port. Fix whatever needs to be taken care of in the fastest time possible and get back out to sea."

Fortunately, S&S has only lost one boat to a fire. However, they have experienced some serious crew accidents. One captain lost a leg when he got tangled in a rope as the nets went overboard. Once the nets hit the water, shrimping doors and chains follow. It's impossible to reverse due to the force of the water. The speed of the boat is also a factor.

Another accident occurred while dropping anchor. The Cabo rope twisted around a crew member but, fortunately, he managed to spin himself free. He later said, "I saw my life being pulled down to the bottom of the ocean." Clinging to the rope with both hands, he somehow pulled his foot out of the rubber deck boot he was wearing. He later said he did not know how he did it. As he fell back against the front side of the wheelhouse in a frightened daze, he saw his white rubber boot wrapped up in the Cabo rope flipped over the front prow of the boat. He sat there drained, unable to move or get to his feet. He had used all of his adrenaline to pry his foot free of the constricting rope.

Moments later the captain and rig man came to his assistance. They helped him to his feet and took him into the boat cabin. After the near-death shock subsided—and as he sat in the galley having dinner with his captain and rig man, he told them that he faintly remembered seeing a winged image swoosh down, grab him under his arm pits and pull him back.

Samuel Snodgrass (painting)

24

THE EUNICE LEE VARNAM FAMILY

> People always said you could eat a meal off the engine floor of
> Daddy's boats.
> Nancy Varnam Sanders

L-R. Lanny, Nancy, Rosemary, Daisy, and Robert

EUNICE VARNAM BROUGHT HIS family to Port Isabel in October of 1949. After moving back and forth between North Carolina and Louisiana, he followed the shrimp and made Texas his home. A member of the Twin City Co-op in Morgan City, Louisiana, he joined others in establishing an office in Port Isabel.

All six of his children have called Port Isabel home since then. A family of three girls and three boys ranged in age from eleven months to fourteen years. Two siblings, Charles and Robert, have passed away. We interviewed the remaining four siblings—Nancy, Daisy, Rosemary, and Lanny—and two of Charles's sons, Chuck and Leif. Nancy's husband, Speck Sanders, came to Port Isabel in the summer of 1951 to work at the oil refinery. He accepted a job here in 1952 following his graduation from TCU (Texas Christian University).

With a span of thirteen years between the oldest and youngest Varnam, their memories covered much of Eunice's life.

Eunice Lee Varnam

Eunice loved the sea and the boats that men built to conquer it. He worked for the Army Corps of Engineers and earned a Second Mate Certification of Competency (a license issued by the International Maritime Organization). The second mate is third in command on ocean-going vessels and is the watch keeper and navigator. However, even the pathway to becoming a first mate paled in comparison to spending hours on the water captaining a fishing boat.

While his family started growing, he switched back and forth between the two career choices. Finally, full time at sea won his heart and soul, and he spent the rest of his working life chasing shrimp around the Gulf of Mexico.

His children's eyes lit up when Daddy returned from sea. His eyes lit whenever he spoke of the sea and his boats.

Eunice and fellow Twin City Co-op member, Ashley Galloway, bought the *Miss Florida*, a wooden-hulled boat. He later bought the *Mary B*, a wooden-hulled, ice boat. He always loved clipper ships, admiring their sleek lines and fascinated by their speed and ability to slice through the water. When he sold the *Mary B*, he built the *Flying Cloud*, a 65-foot, wooden-hulled boat designed with the narrower hull of its namesake clipper. Eunice captained the boat and marveled in its speed and ability to ride stormy swells. He would later build the *Cutty Sark* and the *Sovereign of the Seas*.

He taught his three sons to fish, but only Charles inherited his dad's passion for a life at sea. However, the three boys learned much about the constant work that was a fisherman's life. In port, the crew worked to clean, paint, repair and prepare the boat for the next trip. Once out to sea, they dropped the first net, and then it became a 24-hour, seven-day-a-week job. Lanny attested to his dad's "no special treatment" philosophy for his sons. Eunice expected the same high standards from them as he did the rest of the crew.

Eunice lived his love affair with fishing until he suffered a heart attack at sea. For the first time, his son Charles had to bring the boat through the jetties. Though no longer captaining a boat, Eunice visited the docks every day. Charles took over the management of the company and gradually Eunice's passions turned to land in the form of gardening and wine-making.

Whatever he pursued, he gave it his all and his children and grandchildren have many memories of his "land" years.

In the 1980s, he sold his last boat to Charles.

The Varnam Sons

> Dad never showed us any preference. He treated us like the rest of the crew.

Charles inherited his dad's sea-loving gene. Robert and Lanny didn't. They both chose careers in teaching.

Charles spent his life fishing—alongside his dad and when his dad retired, he assumed the leadership role in the business. He had learned well and when he introduced his sons, Chuck and Leif, to fishing, he taught them the same high standards he learned from his dad. However, they did not have the same enthusiasm for fishing as their father. They sought other jobs. Leif went into teaching and Chuck house painting.

Charles carried a couple of nicknames. When he was in high school in Morgan City, Louisiana, he was full back for the football team the year they won their only state championship. Later, in Port Isabel, he became "Moose." He was a big bruising fullback who plowed over the opposition when he carried the football.

He loved turkey and insisted it was a necessary part of holiday dinners. Lanny would buy Swanson frozen dinners so Charles could celebrate with turkey.

Charles took his sons, Chuck and Leif, on short trips during the summers. As with most kids, both started as headers. Leif started on the *Queen Anitra*, a refrigerated boat named after their younger sister. He remained slow at heading. It took only a couple of fishing trips to know he could never make it a career.

Lanny Varnam

> Fishing was not for me. I remember seasickness, the noise, the smell and the constant motion.

Lanny never adapted to the sea life. He went shrimping because that was the family business. He was expected to contribute his part. He was not alone in this expectation. Most teenage boys in Port Isabel were put on shrimp boats during the summer. They had no summer vacation. They were laborers and an income producing resource for the families.

When we asked for his fondest memories, Lanny laughed. There was no fondness when he spoke of his experiences, but his sense of humor shone through his stories.

What didn't he like? Pretty much everything. When a man is young and he's out to sea for weeks or months, it's easy to envy his friends having fun at home. He missed the parties, the dates and all the special events. After listening to his friends' stories of the many fun times, he wished his father would let him find a job on land during the summer. Lanny eventually got his wish.

Years later after high school and service in the military, he went to college, graduated and became a school teacher. He didn't have to go shrimping any more.

As a kid and young man, Lanny would be sick the first three days. As soon as the boat reached the jetties, the sickness struck. On the *Flying Cloud*, he slept in the engine room where the noise was loud and constant, and the smell of diesel fuel gagged him. Shrimping assaulted his senses—the smells, the noise and the constant motion.

Then there was the work. Once it started, it never stopped. It was constant heading, throwing out trash, cleaning, raising and lowering the nets. There was no downtime and there was no escape from the motion of the boat. He learned to clean the ice hole before the trip and after the shrimp are unloaded.

Once a day, he had to clean the nets, shaking them to get the fish out. He cringed each time he felt the slime and the guts fly against him. By the time he finished, he needed cleaning, too. It was a smelly job and was usually done during the afternoon after the night's catch had been headed and frozen.

His hands never adapted to working with the shrimp. The shrimp contain an acid that burns when it gets in any cut or cracked skin. Cuts, cracks and punctures come with the job. Lanny's hands dried out and after a few days, his dry skin was bloody and painful.

The Varnam Daughters

The whole house lit up when Daddy came home.

With a ten-plus year difference between Nancy and Rosemary, the daughters each knew a different dad in Eunice Varnam.

Nancy, the first child, grew up during her dad's early career. At this point in his life, he had not chosen the profession that would fulfill his dreams. His dad had owned small boats and Eunice learned to fish as a young boy. As a young man, he worked for the Army Corps of Engineers in North Carolina, where he learned the navigation of ocean-going ships. He had already developed a deep bond with the sea. As he bounced back and forth between the two career choices, Nancy developed social skills by attending a different school almost every year. She learned adaptability and the bigger moves to Louisiana and finally to Port Isabel. She arrived here at the age of fourteen, still in the formative years of high school.

She found it harder to adapt to the climate and environmental changes than to a new school. She left the lush greens of the Louisiana bayou country for the semi-arid south Texas weather. She and Daisy both remember the dirt streets, the small homes and fewer people. Fortunately for them, several other Louisiana families moved here about the same time.

Daisy's childhood memories are filled with horses, boats and ferry rides to Padre Island. She was ten when the family moved and she feels fortunate to have had a childhood filled with so much freedom. This was prior to the building of the first Queen Isabella Causeway in 1954. In those days, residents were allowed to keep farm animals on their property. Most families kept chickens for fresh eggs. Some kept and fattened a pig for tamales during the Christmas season. A few families raised goats for milk and cheese. Only a few had cows or horses.

Unless you owned and operated some ranch land on the outskirts of town, people had little use for horses. The only family that ranched was the Barrera family. They allowed friends to ride their horses.

Although they were the first kids on their street, the number grew to seventy-six as other families moved here.

The two remember moving their belongings from Louisiana to Texas in a shrimp truck. The driver had delivered a truckload of shrimp to New York. He then packed the truck with their family belongings and headed back to Port Isabel. They moved to a part of town known as the reservation. At one time, it had been the wireless station and radio tower on a military base. The area is across from the present day Garriga Grade School.

Their dad took both Nancy and Rosemary out on a boat. Nancy stayed in the cabin and did not join in the work. Rosemary went with her dad when they went to pick up the new *Sovereign of the Seas*. She spent the time in air-conditioned comfort.

25

ROBERT VELA

Shrimping is surviving!

ROBERT VELA STARTED SHRIMPING during the summers when he was twelve. His first job was with his dad on the *Bessie Mae*, a single rig boat. His dad encouraged him to become a shrimper because they made more money than most people in Port Isabel. He cleaned the boat, washed the dishes and did anything else his dad requested. At fourteen, he became a header. He knew most of the jobs of the rig man but he didn't know how to cook.

He learned about navigation from Wesley Moore Sr., an expert with the sextant (a navigational tool that measures the angle between a celestial body—such as the sun or moon—and the horizon. It is also called "sighting."). He studied the compass, learning to map routes in all kinds of weather. In the early days before the Fathometer, he learned to use a rope with a rock to search for the bottom of the Gulf floor.

He became a rig man at fifteen and a captain at sixteen. The first boat he captained was a tug boat, the *Patty June*, a forty-footer. Next, the *Rio Bravo*, a seventy-foot shrimp boat. He fished the Bay of Campeche in the winters and began earning a good living. Then he was drafted. He married his sweetheart before he left for Vietnam.

After serving two years, half of it in Vietnam, he returned to shrimping. Although he anticipated a long career, he began having flashbacks from the war. His crew and friends worried that he would go overboard or cause a catastrophe. His friend, Gilbert Groomer, urged him to apply for work at the Laguna Madre Water Department but he was unwilling to take a pay cut. After more flashbacks and three years at sea, he decided to return to school through the GI bill. He earned his GED and took some college courses, earning certification in electronics. He repaired televisions and worked at Outdoor Resorts.

Missing the money, he returned to shrimping. The flashbacks returned and it only took a few months to realize that the problems were not subsiding. He took Gilbert's continuing advice and applied at the water district. Although he took a significant pay cut, he earned his license and became Chief Electrician in his thirty-two-year career.

The years he shrimped were the ones when his family was young and growing. "I was usually in port only about three days before heading back out. My wife did everything."

Like Billy Holland, he never let his two sons near shrimp boats. Always aware that his dad encouraged him to drop out of school, he wanted better for his sons. He urged them to stay in school and get a good education. Both joined the U.S. Marine Corps and served during Desert Storm.

"I never regretted my shrimping days. I made friends and learned how to work hard," Robert recalled. He was in the industry during its growth. Some of his friends, mostly shrimpers who emigrated from Mexico or moved here from Louisiana, achieved wealth. They grew their businesses by steadily building a fleet of boats. Robert loved the days when everybody in Port Isabel had a job.

26

SABINO VILLARREAL

With all my heart, I hope that the shrimping industry doesn't die.

SABINO LOVES ENGINES, BOATS, and shrimping. Like many of his contemporaries, he grew up across the street from the docks. It was second nature for Sabino to hang out there, talking to and running errands for the shrimpers.[1]

---

1 Most kids picked up a few nickels and quarters by running errands.

After graduating from high school, Sabino enlisted in the army. He married Lupita when he was still in the service. After his military discharge, Sabino returned to Port Isabel and began working as a diesel mechanic and salesman for a local parts store.

One of Sabino's dreams in life was to own a shrimp boat. For years, he and Lupita saved their money. When they had enough for a down payment, he found a used shrimp boat he liked and could afford. The local bank gave them a loan—and Sabino was a shrimp boat owner at last.

Things went well. He made the payments on time and saved more money. The bank was happy. He and Lupita were happy. The future looked bright. They sold their starter home and bought a bigger house in a better part of town. They bought another boat and his dream grew bigger. A few years later, the SBA approved him for another loan and they bought a third boat.

Then suddenly, his luck turned. On a fishing trip, Sabino took out two boats and served as captain on one. The shrimping was good as they stayed just outside Mexican waters. The productive trip turned sour as Mexican gun boats chased, caught and confiscated both boats. As per custom, they took the catch, stripped the boats and levied a fine on them.

Although Sabino was successfully building his business, he didn't have large cash reserves. The Mexicans wanted seventy-five thousand for both boats plus he'd have to repair and restock them. He appealed to his congressman for help, but never received a return call. Although the U.S. agreed that he had been captured in international waters, his attorneys advised him not to try to get them back. Unable to make his SBA loan payments, he lost the third boat.

The straw that broke the camel's back for Sabino came when a crew of Mexican shrimpers brought one of his boats to Port Isabel for repairs. It was an in-your-face reminder of what he had lost. They were working *his* boat for *their* benefit. He notified local law enforcement officials that his boat was in port and that he wanted to take possession of it.

Law enforcement told Sabino that he could not do it. His boat now belonged to Mexico. They further told him that if he boarded the boat to take it back, they would arrest him. In fact, the local sheriff kept deputies on the dock to make sure he did not follow through with his intent of taking back his boat. They told him they were trying to avoid an international incident with Mexico.

Sabino is rightfully proud of his years at sea and on land. His connection to shrimping runs deep and wide. He worked as crew and captain, owned and lost three boats, worked as a diesel mechanic—and spent the last twenty-eight years in the parts department at Bodden and Caddell, Inc.

Sabino shared his love of engines. The company's boats house Caterpillar 3408s, a V-8 diesel marine engine with up to 520 horsepower. According to Sabino, it is the most dependable motor on the market. "It lasts longer and gets twelve-to-eighteen gallons per hour." Their boats use Isuzu diesel generator motors.

Over those years, he saw diesel fuel prices rise from twelve cents to more than three dollars per gallon. He watched the downward slide of the shrimping industry,

followed by the decline of people who called Port Isabel home.

"It makes me sad. At one time there were two-
to-four-hundred boats and six or seven fish houses
around here. Now we have about fifty boats and only
four houses."

27

FRANCESCO VOLTAGGIO

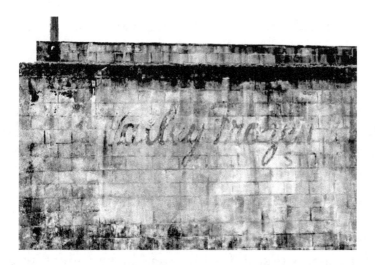

BORN OF ITALIAN IMMIGRANT parents, Francesco grew up to be a successful businessman in the Rio
Grande Valley and in Mexico. A truly multicultural
man, he adapted easily to different cultures. With an
entrepreneurial spirit and strong business sense, he
founded and built the largest shrimp processing business in the Port Isabel/Brownsville area.

His parents, Vincenzo and Vincenza, emigrated
from Italy around 1900. They settled in Newark, NJ.
Francesco was the sixth of eight children. His father
died when he was four and his mother raised the children alone. Francesco became Frank when his teachers

changed his name. He learned English in school but continued to speak Italian at home.

He first went to work at the age of six, shining shoes in his uncle's tailor shop. As a teenager, he worked in the ice cream business for another uncle. As a young adult, he met his future. He found a job at the Fulton Fish Market in New York. He soon began buying trucks to transport fresh vegetables from Florida.

He met his wife, Lorene Davidson, in Florida. They married and had two daughters, Wanda and Virginia. Frank moved his family to Orange, Texas, to learn the shrimping industry. Over the next four years, he learned about the fishing, processing and sale of shrimp.

In the late 1940s, he bought a processing plant in Tampico, Mexico. He loved the business and the Mexican culture. Business flourished and all was well until the Mexican government claimed the business. According to Virginia, "The business was thriving so much that the Mexican government decided to take over this business owned by a U.S. citizen. Frank and several of the men working for him were lucky enough to get away from the soldiers by jumping on board a large vessel and making their way into the Gulf of Mexico, headed for the coast of Texas."

Frank lost everything. Adding to their troubles, their escape coincided with a major storm in the Gulf. If Frank hadn't bought a mine sweeper from the U.S. Government and turned it into a shrimping boat, his story may have had a different ending.

He went back to Brownsville and in 1949, established a processing plant in one of the old barracks at Fort Brown. It was the beginning of the city's shrimp processing industry. He bought shrimp from Mexico, brought them into the U.S., processed and boxed them in his brand name, *Valley Pride*—and shipped them to Detroit and New York. He continued using *Valley Pride* throughout his career.

In 1950 he moved his family to Brownsville. He met Frank and Oliver Clark at a seafood conference. Within two years, they joined forces and established Valley Frozen Foods. They moved the company to Port Isabel and bought several acres along the port entry. Both Frank and Oliver lived in Brownsville and drove back and forth to work in the Port Isabel facility.

At the same time (around 1953-1954), the port built Brownsville Harbor for fishing boats. It was the first harbor in the U.S. devoted to fishing boats. They welcomed shrimpers arriving from Louisiana. As the Port Isabel industry grew, their business flourished.

Valley Frozen Foods was the first in the Valley to use nitrogen for quick freezing. They became the largest operation in Port Isabel. It was a market-driven economy and everyday New York and Chicago buyers would set the price of shrimp. Valley Frozen Foods would learn the price and pass it on other companies in Port Isabel.

When shrimp boats arrived at their dock, the company sounded a horn to alert people that the plant needed workers. During the peak season, Valley Frozen Foods employed 300 people, doubling their normal size. They divided work by gender. Women headed shrimp and sorted them by size as they moved along a conveyor belt. Men worked the heavier jobs, moving the boxed shrimp into the freezer and loading them onto conveyor belts.

The company moved into the fishing side of the business when they began buying their own boats. Most of their fleet carried the Valley name, such as *Valley Star*, *Valley Sun*, etc. During the 1960s, the company operated the largest privately-owned shrimp fleet in the area.

Soon competitors began opening plants. Sometimes they hired Valley Frozen Foods to custom pack privately branded product for them. The company secured a U.S. Army contract for shrimp. Although the Army paid well, they made demands, including an Army representative on site to monitor the entire process.

Frank's brothers, Antonio and Morris, had come to work for them in the mid 1950s. Tony was an accountant and became the office manager. Morris worked with Frank in operations until he set up his own unloading and dock facility in Port Isabel in the late 1960s. In the early 1970s, Frank's business partner, Oliver Clark, decided to move his family back to Alabama. Frank bought out his interest.

After Oliver left, Frank got the itch to invest in Mexico again. He connected with an operation in Tampico and Campeche. This time he partnered with Mexican citizens. They bought all their shrimp from two Mexican plants. This worked for a few years until the government took control of the industry. They nationalized the boats and the industry. It had been good while it lasted. Throughout his life, Frank loved the Mexican culture and the people.

As Frank grew older, he wanted more family members in the business. Wanda's husband worked for him for several years. Two of Frank's brothers tried it but didn't like it. Virginia's husband became president of the company but when the industry experienced a steady decline, Frank convinced him to transition into another line of work.

Frank sold the business in the 1980s. The Valley Frozen Foods building still stands in Port Isabel. Today its name on the outside wall is faint.

Frank believed in community. He served as president of the Texas Shrimp Association and as president of the Shrimp Producers Association, as well as president of both Kiwanis and the Propeller Club. He and Lorene belonged to the Serape Club where authentic Mexican costumes were won at social events.

28

MIKE ZIMMERMAN

> Shrimping wasn't for me.

IN THE LATE 1940S, Mike's grandfather came to the Valley coast to fish. He lived in McAllen and worked in the oil industry until an economic slump. He liked Port Isabel, stayed, opened a small store and purchased property in Port Isabel where he built a railway near the old Yacht Club. His sons, Walter and Bill, (Mike's father) joined the family business.

The family transitioned from boat repair to shrimping and finally to boat building. In the 1950s, they repaired boats. After they hauled in and repaired a boat for a local fisherman who couldn't pay the bill, they accepted the boat as payment. The boat had been used for red snapper fishing. They converted it to a shrimping boat and renamed it the *Vera Cruz*. That began what would eventually turn into a fleet of twenty boats.

Mike grew up in the family business—building and repairing shrimp boats. He worked for his dad and uncle during his school years. His job wasn't inside a nice air-conditioned office answering the telephone or running office errands. Instead he worked in the scorching summer heat doing the most menial of labor jobs. He shoveled mud and sludge into a wheel barrel and pushed it to a disposal pit for hours. He picked up and removed trash the railway workers cast aside while doing their job. He earned the workers sympathy as they watched him work like a burro all day long under the hot sun. His father, who showed no sympathy, had his reasons for working Mike the way he did. He wanted to teach him the business from the ground up. Mike learned well and eventually ran the business after his dad retired.

He attempted to learn the shrimping part of the business by working on board a shrimp boat. That didn't last long however. While most first-time crew members take two to three days to get used to being out at sea, Mike didn't. He quickly learned that being a shrimper on a boat was not for him. He suffered from seasickness the entire time he was on the water.

However, the time he spent on a working shrimp boat taught him something. He developed an appreciation for the work of a shrimper. Working on a shrimp boat is one of the most challenging jobs anyone can do.

After he graduated from college, he returned home to join his dad and uncle. In the 1960s, the Zimmermans built their first boat—a steel-hulled, seventy-foot-long vessel with ice storage. Soon they began building boats for other fishermen. They expanded during the 1970s and 1980s, growing from about twelve boats a year to around twenty.

At one time, they employed more than 100 people, making them a major Port Isabel employer. During the 1970s–1980s, they produced more than 250 boats. They also sold fuel and supplies.

The family kept a fleet of seventeen-to-twenty boats during this period. Each boat regularly carried a three-man crew. At the peak of the industry, two or three extra headers would be added to each crew.

"In the early days, our boats burned eighteen-to-twenty gallons of diesel fuel per hour. A boat would need to carry seventeen-thousand gallons. Even at seventeen cents per gallon, it was a huge expense at the time," Mike recalled. "Boats are more efficient now. They have better engines and netting."

The last boat they built in the 1990s cost $400,000. Today that would be over $1,000,000. No new boats are built today due to the limited entry laws in Texas, the high costs, and banks reluctance to lend money.

29

THOMAS GARCIA

Zimco Marine

THOMAS GARCIA, A BROWNSVILLE native, works for Zimco and shared his enthusiasm for the shrimping industry. As he guided me on a tour around the property, shrimpers unloaded a boat just in from the Gulf.

We watched the shrimp boxes being loaded on a conveyor belt, weighed, counted and placed on a pallet. A forklift then loaded the pallets onto a truck. Once on the truck, the shrimp is taken to the freezer house for processing and storage. From there the shrimp is sold to buyers. These buyers then sell and distribute the shrimp to other markets throughout the United States.

Zimco runs a fleet of fifteen boats. The boats all have the named Cruz (which means Cross). When the Zimmerman brothers, Bill and Walter first got started owning and operating shrimp boats, they began with a boat named *Vera Cruz*, which means "True Cross" in Spanish. They acquired the boat off the boat railway they operated in Port Isabel. The railway is where shrimp boats are brought for major repairs. They are loaded on steel rails much like the ones trains run on. They pull the boat and lift it completely out of the water into a work station. There the boat is secured and readied for repairs. Railway work usually involves anything having to do with the hull of the boat.

Every few years boats are taken out of the water and placed on these rails for maintenance. Under normal circumstances, water inevitably gets inside the hull and causes damage. The constant pounding from the sea leads to leaks. They may start as a hairline crack, but if not fixed, the breach grows longer and wider. Eventually, the pump can't keep up with the seepage. So, to prevent the unthinkable disaster of sinking at sea, each boat must be periodically railed and repaired—and the thousands of barnacles growing on the hull removed. Railways are also used for sandblasting, painting and other maintenance procedures.

The repairs to the *Vera Cruz* apparently were too many and too costly. Its owner did not have the money and decided to sign over ownership to Bill and Walter. Soon after assuming ownership of the *Vera Cruz*, the Zimmerman brothers acquired the *Salinas Cruz*. After that they began to build their own shrimp boats. Every new boat they added to their growing fleet carried with it the name of Cruz. In addition to operating the fleet, they repair their own boats, weave the netting, and house their own fuel. Zimco is owned and operated by Walter's descendants—one of the Zimmerman brothers.

The company sells its shrimp through its subsidiary, Texas Gold Shrimp.

30

INCARNACION "CHONITO" DELGADO

The Net Mending Men

SHRIMPING AND FISHING ARE not possible without net men. These are the guys who make it possible for shrimpers to catch shrimp. They are an essential part of the industry. They show up at their small net shops daily to make, mend and repair ripped and mangled nets. One never knows what hazards lay at the bottom of the sea. All shrimpers keep maps and charts of sites where other shrimpers have reported getting their nets caught and torn by debris or large rocks. They avoid these sites by fishing around them. Boat owners and captains absolutely hate it when they rip open a brand new net. They lose shrimp and money. Depending on the size of the tear, they could lose hundreds of dollars' worth of shrimp during one single drag not to mention the cost of the repair.

Most captains and many rig men know how to repair small rips. They inspect their nets daily for tears as part of their job. If they find any tears they are able to repair they do so. When they find big rips that require the expertise of a net man, they take the damaged net off its rigging and replace it with a new one. All boats carry with them several extra nets for situations like this.

Captains especially hate it when a big tear happens during prime night trawling time. They have to stop fishing completely. They pull in all of their rigging, drop anchor and proceed to change out the damaged net with a new one. The exchange time takes hours and they can lose the rest of the night trawl. Again, lost time and money and net repair costs cut into their profits. After the frustrating time spent repairing their nets, the captain enters the new danger site on his maps. The entry will have the exact longitude and latitude coordinates for future reference. He will also get on the side band radio and let the rest of the fleet know, that unfortunately for him and his boat, they discovered a new tear site.

The rest of the fleet captains will in turn enter the reported hazard in their maps and pass the information on to other boats. The practice of reporting every tear site found to the entire fleet is common courtesy.

There have been many shrimp boat net makers and menders in Port Isabel's shrimping history. Two that come to mind are a father and son duo. Together these two generations of net men serviced boats and captains for more than fifty years. They are Incarnacion Delgado Sr. and Incarnacion Delgado Jr. Incarnacion Sr. was called Chon, short for Incarnacion and Jr. was called Chonito. The father taught the son who continued making and mending shrimping nets for many years after his father retired from the trade. Their net shop was located right on the dock water front between Twin City Co-op and the WBP fish houses.

Beside the obvious purpose of repairing nets, the shop served as a gathering place for men, a kind of informal social club. Captains came to drop off their nets for repair and lingered to talk about the shrimping trip and how the nets were torn. Chonito would in turn give them some news about the town happenings while they were gone. They talked about politics, the weather, the wins and losses of the local high school football team and all sports. Everyone's opinion mattered and all understood that it was okay to disagree without losing friendships. At the end of the day everyone went home with no grudges held.

The shop became a place to play cards. Small stakes poker games were a daily event. The radio was always on, tuned to KGBT, a Spanish station that played Mexican conjunto and Tejano music and broadcast the news in Spanish. The shop had a smoker, a small gas stove, a refrigerator and freezer. It served great tasting barbeque, finger-licking fried fish and shrimp, countless delicious stews and soups. Most of the time, when people drove by Chonitos, the prevailing southeast breeze carried a savoring whiff of the day's menu.

The shop was a long-shot gun structure made out of wood and corrugated sheet metal siding. It had no air-conditioning, but somehow it was never hot. A big industrial fan situated on the water side of the building sucked in the water-cooled air off the channel and funneled it in one end and out the other. Several windows ran the length of each side of the shop. They had no screens and were propped and held open with 2x4 inch boards. At the end of the day, the boards were removed and the windows latched from the inside.

Pesky flies and other bugs were never a problem. Perhaps the smell of the nets kept them away. Nets are dipped in a solution mixture of tar and other chemicals after they are made. Apparently the flies and mosquitoes didn't like the tarry smell. Chonito always worked in a sleeveless undershirt and appreciated the fact that the unique odor of his trade kept the bugs away. They didn't sting or bother him. He had no time to shoo them away. His skilled hands were too busy pulling and tugging twine into perfect net mesh. He cut, sewed and mended all day long, except for his lunch break. He could mend, think and talk at the same time and always engaged in the conversation at hand. Like his visitors, he too had strong opinions on the issues being discussed.

Whenever a captain dropped off his net at the shop to get mended, they told him when they needed the nets. So Chonito always had deadlines and he met them. If he told a captain he would have his nets ready to go for his next fishing trip, he kept his word. When the captain returned, his nets were ready.

Chonito welcomed everyone who came to his shop. If someone was hungry, he ate. If he needed a few dollars, fine. Good advice was always free. But the best thing about Chonito's net shop was the gathering of men in an informal social setting with one thing in common. Everyone was in one way or another intertwined within the meshes of Port Isabel's shrimping industry and Chonito Delgado, the net man, was its mender.

31

ROBERTO T. GARCIA

ROBERTO WAS IN THE Navy and fought the Japanese in the South Pacific during WWII. When he volunteered, he was married to Magdalena Holland and had two young daughters, Maria Magdalena and Sara. Because of his family, he could have gotten a stateside assignment supporting the troops overseas. He chose instead to fight.

After WWII, Roberto returned home to Port Isabel. He went shrimping. The industry was in a transition period, moving from Bay to Gulf fishing, from the Padre Island beaches to far offshore. He fished for a few years. He was the captain of the *Alamo*, the first steel-hull boat in Port Isabel. After saving enough money to build his family a home, he found work on land. He became a longshoreman at the Port Isabel / San Benito Navigation District. Large cargo ships were coming in from Central America with loads of bananas, pineapples and citrus. They needed men to unload the cargo, place it on rail cars, and send it inland up north. Roberto did this until the late 1950s when began working with Urban Renewal, a federal housing redevelopment program.

The program went into the Mexiquito section of Port Isabel south of the railroad to South Shore Drive. At the time, Mexiquito neighborhood residences consisted of small shanties or substandard homes. There were no paved streets and all the residences had outhouses. The area lacked zoning laws. There were cantinas everywhere in the neighborhood. People kept pigs, chickens and goats in their backyards. Keeping livestock and poultry for domestic use was acceptable but the backyards in Mexiquito measured no more than twenty-five feet by twenty-five.

This and the outhouses made for unsanitary conditions. The city asked the federal government for help. Fortunately, the government agreed. They gave the city financial assistance. Utilizing eminent domain, Port Isabel purchased the residents' property at market value. All the shanties and cantinas were leveled. Citizens received low-term, low-interest financing to rebuild the neighborhood with modern brick veneer homes. The streets were all paved. They had indoor plumbing. The lots that once before were twenty-five wide by one hundred deep were now fifty feet wide by one hundred twenty feet deep.

Later, in life. Roberto said, that he was grateful to the shrimping industry. It allowed him to build a fine home for his wife and children. But the most gratifying job he ever had was working for Urban Renewal. He was placed in a position to help his old neighborhood transform from a shanty quarter of town beset by cantinas on every street corner to a nice modern livable area. The modernization greatly improved the quality of life for many of his friends and neighbors.

32

ALBERT ALEGRIA

Port Isabel School Boys of Summer

ALBERT ALEGRIA WAS A typical Port Isabel school boy. As soon as he was old enough, he spent his summer vacations on a shrimp boat. That's how boys spent their summers; working on a boat heading shrimp. His one exception occurred the summer he was twelve. His mother Sofia was a single parent at the time. She felt

Albert was old enough to work and contribute towards the household income. She sent him with one of his uncles to work the migrant farm fields up north.

The following summer Albert told his mother he didn't want to go back up north with his Uncle Chino to work in the migrant farm fields. The next day his mother said. "Okay you don't have to go work up north if you don't want to. You're going shrimping with your Uncle Uvaldo. I already spoke with him, and he agreed that you can go with him on his boat and work as a header."

Albert did as his mother told him and went shrimping. He continued to shrimp during the summers through high school. In fact, he continued shrimping summers during his college years while he was at the University of Houston. When the spring semester ended, Albert would ask one of his college friends to drive him from Houston to Galveston. His then stepfather, Captain Tomas Torres, would be waiting for him with his boat tied to the dock. Albert would hop on board with his pillow case (the shrimper's version of a sea bag) stuffed with his fishing clothes and off they went.

Albert paid for his college this way. After graduating with a Bachelor's degree in kinesiology and biology, Albert found a land job and never went shrimping again. Sofia, his mother, told him years later that money was not the reason she wanted him to work in the summer. She worked hard herself and could manage financially. When Albert and his sisters were children, she worked at one of the shrimp processing plants. Years later, she married Tomas Torres, a shrimp boat captain. Every time Tomas came in from shrimping, he brought Sofia fifty to one hundred pounds of shrimp for their home freezer. Sofia sold the shrimp to local restaurants and friends to help sustain the family. She saved as much of the money from the sale of the shrimp as she could. During the Catholic Lenten season, she made extra money by chopping and selling cactus pods in pint-size zip lock baggies.

Sofia wanted him to work with his uncles to learn how to work hard. The experience would help him later in life when he grew to adulthood. She was right. Albert indeed learned how to work hard. He developed and still maintains a strong work ethic. He is a respected educator, founder and President of a Teachers' Union, as well as a successful rancher and land owner.

Albert back in the day

33

MANUEL BARROSO

LIKE MOST TEEN-AGED BOYS, Jose "Manuel" Barroso worked as a header on the Zimmermans' boats, under Captain Agapito Villarreal and rig man Federico Fierro. The old saying, 'the third time's the charm,' fits Manuel's experience who after only three fishing trips realized that he preferred cooking to catching.

"It wasn't for me," he said.

Tourists and locals alike celebrate his choice. Over the years, Manuel owned several restaurants with his mother on South Padre Island and in Port Isabel. He currently operates *Manuel's* on Maxan Street with his son Frank. The eatery draws patrons from all over the world and maintains a reputation for some of the best food in the Valley.

Although shrimping was not for him, he said his uncles Juan Sanchez and Lupe Sanchez had successful careers in the industry.

34

TWO BOYS OF TEN

The story of two young boys who were taken to sea during
the summer.

Two boys of ten were Eddie and me
I from November, He in February
And does comes the summer,
When both were taken to sea
To fish and to shrimp, Eddie and me.
I emptied my stomach again and again,
Hanging my spinning head over the railing,
Of the 65-foot trawler named the Southern Glory.
A wooden shrimp boat, scaling the front end
Of, ten-foot seas, then sliding down the back side
Of each wave, before starting its next climb, and
Sliding, sometimes skidding, back down again.
A never-ending torturous roller coaster ride
I could not get off from.
It would be twenty days and nights before
We would return back to Port Isabel,
Safe to the tranquil waters of the Brazos de Santiago Pass,
And the welcoming arms of the Laguna Madre.

Eddie brought me some crushed ice in a tin cup.
He had seen my sickness and felt compassion for me.
He got the ice from the hull belly of the boat
Where just a few hours before was tied to the dock.
We had filled its bins with one hundred,
One hundred-pound bars of frozen ice blocks.
Crushed and grinned into flakey shavings of
Snow cone snow used to keep the netted
Catch of Brown and white Gulf shrimp fresh.
"Eat this!" he said, keep eating it until you finish it."
"When you're finished with it, I will bring you some more."
"It won't make you feel any better but at least
You will have something in your stomach until
The sea sickness passes."
"Thank you, primo" I replied.
I watched him walk to the prow of the wave bucking boat.
He grabbed the anchor Cabo-rope with both hands
And began to imitate a bronco busting cowboy.
With each jerking lift of giant wave after
constant giant wave.
I stayed behind on the stern deck, asking myself
in private anguish;
When will this torment feeling end? "Keep your eyes
to the horizon!"
Eddie shouted back at me, "Sometimes that
helps the dizziness!"
As he straddled the anchor, facing forward,
riding the rough sea.
The Captain, Uncle Joe, steered the vessel steady ahead.

Crashing against and cutting into the angry face of each

Tall foam crested swell that challenged our exploration

Of its body; the clear emerald water of the Gulf of Mexico.

He protectively watched both of us and thought it natural

How life and fate sets the course for two boys

and their future.

One sick as can be, heaving green lime vile out of

his aching belly.

Saying to himself, "What am I doing here?"

The other, content, standing at the front point of the boat

Anxiously waiting for the next big wave to come

tubing over him.

Shaking, the salty sea spray off his wet body like

a happy Labrador

Retriever shakes his coat free of water after a swim.

The summer did finally pass, that year when we were ten.

The fall school term soon followed, and so to my studies

I eagerly returned, I was now soon to be eleven, strong

and sun tanned.

Eddie decided he was not enrolling for classes anymore.

He told his father so. he said, "a sea man was what

he wanted to be".

His father said, "That's fine with me, but

remember this son,

From this day forward, you shall belong to her,

the sea I mean.

For she is a very possessive and jealous lover and will never

set you free."

If you're lucky, she will let you live to be a crippled
old man in constant
Pain, the result of all the many broken bones and
over excreted muscles.
Retiring to a life of sitting in on a rocking chair, rolling yourself
back and forth
On land, telling your grandchildren gathered
around you, sea stories
Or she will love you so much that she may
someday or some night
Take you deep to the bottom and keep you there forever,
just for her.
"That's fine" said Eddie; to his father... "I love the sea.
Chasing and catching shrimp, that's the life for me,
Schooling and school books, he said, weren't for he.
The trade winds and tall rolling waves kept calling said he,
A Shrimper, a Rig man, a Captain, that's
the future for me".
Other summers followed, and I returned to the sea
To shrimp with Uncle Joe, and my cousin Eddie.
Each time, he fed me crushed ice for my sickness
I taught him some reading and writing skills, too.
He taught me the compass, the fathoms, currents,
Winds, latitude lines, longitude lines and some
net mending, plus
He pointed to the endless constellations of flickering
stars at night.
"There is the little dipper, over there the big dipper, that
there is Venus,

That over there is Mars, Venus and Mars, love each
other he said.
Just like the Moon and the Sun love each other, but
They can only love each other from a distance, never close.
"Amor de lejos." They can never come together.
If they do, they will fight, kinda like cats and dogs fight.
There is the North Star. She will always let you know
Where south, east and west are, this way you will always
Be able to find you way." Eddie always knew
Where he was, at least when he was out at sea.
I went off to college, after my eighteenth summer.
Eddie sailed to the Bay of Campeche following the shrimp.
For the next four years, we saw each other only a few times.
I was busy studying, Eddie busy, sailing the Gulf of Mexico.
Shrimping and making every port of call from
Tampico to Key West.
Four years later, Captain Eddie attended
my college graduation.
We shook hands; his were big, rough and calloused,
Mine were soft, not as big. He said he was proud of me
I told him, I too was proud of him for becoming
a Lord at sea.
More years passed, I as an academic,
Eddie as a sea voyaging Captain.
He saved his money to purchase his dream.
A dream, he dreamed about during his many
Sleepless nights, navigating and steering
His way through the long dark lonely nights of
Shrimp season after shrimp season.

He bought, his very own shrimp boat,
Along with a brand-new wool pea coat
To wear during the cold winters at sea.
I went to the christening of his boat. The Lady Cora Lee,
A seventy-four-foot-long steel hull trawler fully rigged.
We shook hands; his were still big rough and calloused
Mine still soft. I told him how proud I was of him.
I brought him a gift to wear
A Captains' hat for his head and good aura.
I asked him to take me along on his vessel's maiden voyage
He agreed.
No sooner had we cleared the jetty, entering the
wide-open sea
When the contents of my stomach began to churn
inside of me.
Moments later, what do I see? Eddie extending the
same old tin cup
Filled to the top, with crushed ice. He said he had
saved it for me.
He knew, I would be back some day to sail with
him once again.
Even, if it was just for fun, so he kept the cup, I took it
from his hand.
So, there we were, two grown men, who once were
lads of ten.
One was called by the deep blue sea, the other
moored to land.
Each destined to chart their own separate course in life,
Perhaps by fate, perhaps not, no matter, two blood brothers

Growing old together, nautical miles apart, my cousin
… Eddie and me.

Rudy H Garcia Summer 2010

35

THE BLESSING OF
THE FLEET

Bountiful catch! Lots of shrimp!
Reverend Mark Watters

THE BLESSING OF THE Fleet is held at the beginning of the shrimping season each year. Father Mark Watters gives the blessing, wishing the shrimpers a successful and safe trip.

In the past, the local Catholic Bishop was taken on board a shrimp boat to bless the fleet before the start of the season. The boats then started their long procession, lined one behind another out to sea. The Blessing of the Fleet dates back many years for the Port Isabel and Brownsville shrimpers. The bishop offers a special Mass, for their safety and for a bountiful harvest.

During those years, the financial benefits derived from shrimping kept Port Isabel economically healthy. Virtually every working age resident had a job. Unemployment did not exist. Men who worked as shrimpers often took their teenage sons along as crew members, especially during the summer shrimp harvest.

B. B. Burnell, Port Isabel mayor from 1941–1945, knew how badly people needed community during World War II. The July 4th Shrimp Fiesta became the town's highlight and lasted many years after the war had ended. Many locals still remember the street parade with its marching band, decorated floats that celebrated all things shrimp-related. Spectators lined the street waiting to catch a glimpse of the Shrimp Fiesta Queen and her Court of Dukes and Duchesses. The celebration culminated that evening in the Grand Finale of the Fiesta, a parade of decorated shrimp boats, followed by a street dance.

Owners had scrubbed and polished their boats before decking them out in Red, White and Blue. The celebration radiated American pride. Children and adults wanted to ride on one of the decorated boats. Families crowded aboard, filling every deck space inside and outside of the cabin. The fog horns blared and the music entertained.

The menu offered hot dogs, sandwiches, potato salad and soda pop for the kids or beer for the grown-ups. The boats lined up and toured the deep water of the banana docks. It was a big gigantic floating picnic! People came from out of town to enjoy and view the spectacle of Port Isabel's flotilla. After circling the banana docks, the parade of boats procceded to the Brownsville Ship Channel. They turned east towards the Brazos de Santiago Pass and continued out past the end of the jetties before turning back to end the day at the fish house docks. Spectators lined the banks of the Navigation district to enjoy the picturesque shrimp boats.

The Parade

On Shrimp Fiesta Days, every little girl became a beautiful seaside princess and every little boy, a gallant captain.

Rita Alaniz Garcia and Albert Alegria

36

CULTURE CLASH

The Vietnamese Shrimpers in the 1970s

> The Vietnamese and Port Isabel residents never blended. It
> was a cultural clash.
> Linda Sagnes

IN 1975, AT THE end of the Vietnam War, many South
Vietnamese refugees immigrated to the United States.
With the help of the Catholic Diocese of Brownsville,
one-hundred-and-fifty arrived in Port Isabel. Charles
Isabel (a local shrimp boat and fish house owner)
planned to employ them on his shrimp boats. They
settled in the area known as The Harvey Courts. These
courts were once located between Queen Isabel Blvd.
and West Rail Road Street, across from Jimmy's Bait
Stand and Marina on the Port Isabel Channel, and
Bridge Street, behind where the Mexiquito Restaurant
is now located.

The Harvey Courts were small efficiency units
constructed of orange red brick. Each unit had a car-
port attached, large enough to fit one car. The courts
were built to serve as a place for tourists and sports

fisherman. Port Isabel's proximity to the southern part of the Laguna Madre had become a popular destination for sporting fisherman from different parts of the country; mostly from the midwest and northern states. They came seeking the thrill of hooking and landing big fat speckled trout, strong pulling red fish and the powerful fighting tarpon. They also came fishing for offshore fun is search of giants such as marlin, sail fish and tuna, at a time when game fish were plentiful.

The living area for Harvey's Courts was approximately two hundred-to-two-hundred-and-fifty square feet. The units didn't have bed rooms. They had a shower, a small kitchenette and combined dining room, and a living area barely big enough for two beds and a sofa. The cramped accommodations didn't allow comfortable living for more than two people.

The South Vietnamese families that were brought to the Harvey Courts typically included the father, mother and two-to-four children. Many families included one and two grandparents. Imagine eight people living in two-hundred-square-foot area.

The Catholic Church welcomed them, setting up a special Vietnamese Mass. The Point Isabel School District did their best to integrate the children. They made instructional accommodations by including them in their bilingual education program. They hired Vietnamese and English-speaking teacher assistants to help with the children's instruction and translation. They were also used as school-to-parent liaisons, but a serious language and cultural barrier still existed.

The student population spoke English and Spanish and now a third language, along with the Vietnamese Culture, was introduced into the school and town community. The residents of Port Isabel didn't welcome their new neighbors. Many local men, in particular the bay fisherman and shrimpers, felt that the Vietnamese were going to take their jobs.

Other Port Isabel men involved in the shrimping industry resented the fact that the United States government provided no help to them, but facilitated the means for the Vietnamese to acquire fully equipped shrimp boats. The government also provided them with a fuel supply, so that they would be able to operate and fish.

The local shrimpers knew intellectually that government officials were trying to give the refugees a kick start in a new world. Noe Lopez, a long time shrimper, remembers the bitterness it caused among the locals. The resentment towards the Vietnamese was fueled by the fact that year after year, local fishermen struggled to pay back bank loans after shrimping season. In some cases, various shrimpers who used their boats as collateral to secure a bank loan lost their boats for failure to repay the loan note.

Their different lifestyle created the biggest problem. The Vietnamese preferred to fish during the day. They wanted to go out in the morning and return back home in the afternoon. This method ran contrary to the local shrimping practice of going out far into the Gulf of Mexico to fish for weeks (night fishing) at a time before returning back to port. They liked taking their wives with them as crew members returning at the end of the day to spend their nights at home.

Going out to sea on a boat to work for an extended period was foreign to them. They were used to drying fish and shrimp for storage and consumption at a later date. They began to dry their fish on top of the Harvey Courts roofs. The strong pungent smell of dried fish would be picked up by the constant prevailing sea breeze. The winds carried the unpleasant stench throughout the surrounding neighborhood into people's homes. Air conditioning was almost nonexistent in Port Isabel during those years.

The Vietnamese didn't own automobiles. They walked everywhere. Port Isabel is a small town and everything is within walking distance (even today). The two cultures made no effort to blend and accept each other's diversity. They didn't and couldn't communicate much at all. The only times they spoke to one another was when they went into the local stores to purchase food items they needed. Even than the communication was distorted.

Although the Vietnamese, Mexican-American, and local Anglo communities were family-oriented, the many differences in their lifestyles and the unwillingness to get to know each other doomed any possibility of a successful integration.

Within the year, the one-hundred-and-fifty Vietnamese left Port Isabel and resettled in Sea Drift, a small fishing village on Galveston Bay south of Houston. Again, as it had happened in Port Isabel, a culture clash occurred. The reasons for the clash in Sea Drift were much the same as in Port Isabel. The Vietnamese resisted making the rapid transition to the American way of life, or at least, that was the perception of the locals.

The fishermen in the Sea Drift region also felt the same as the Port Isabel fisherman did when the Vietnamese first arrived to live among them.

They felt the Vietnamese new comers were going to cut into their livelihood, causing financial hardship for them and their families. After a couple of years of antagonistic relationships, violent incidences broke out between the two communities. The national spotlight came to Sea Drift with a murder trial. After two Vietnamese were acquitted of killing a white fishermen, racism raised its ugly head. The KKK became involved, wanting vengeance for what they believed was an injustice. The not-guilty verdict further inflamed the Texas residents, especially the residents around Sea Drift. In an effort to prevent further and more serious problems, the federal government ordered the KKK to suspend their activities in 1981. The tension slowly began to lessen. Almost forty years later, the Vietnamese community is fully blended into the local Texas culture. They are prosperous and contribute economically. Their children and grandchildren identify as Americans.

The troubles that began to surface for all coastal fishermen exaggerated the situation. Costs rose, imports grew and profits diminished. However, as time went by and a new normal settled in, the Vietnamese became an integral part of the industry.

37

ACCIDENTS

Shrimping is dangerous work.

MOST SHRIMPERS HAVE STORIES of injuries and even deaths at sea. Storms, cables and rigging and lack of attention can cause accidents. Port Isabel is a small community and most shrimpers know each other. They often share the same stories.

Some captains blame drinking, drugs and carelessness for many of the accidents at sea. Lack of attention is also a factor. An accident can occur the second a shrimper takes his attention off the job at hand.

Billy Holland recalled only one accident on his boat, a crew member broke his leg. Robert Vela told of a man who fell overboard on a boat in the fleet. The boats circled around until they rescued him. It can be difficult to sight and then rescue someone in the water. The boats have their nets out and must maneuver around in such a way that they don't tangle the nets.

Sandalio Alaniz considers himself lucky. He fell and cracked his ribs twice. Once a rope hit a crew member in the ribs, threw him across the boat and knocked him out. Sandalio resuscitated him and took him to the doctor when they reached port. Luckily, his injuries were minor.

Mares Martinez remembered three incidents. He spoke of a friend who fell overboard and was lost. On one of his trips, Mares turned his boat around and rescued a twenty-year-old crew member who had fallen off another boat. He also recalled a crew member who fell overboard but was able to swim back to the boat.

Noe Lopez recalls a failed effort to rescue a man who had fallen overboard during a storm. Noe's boat and several others circled around to help find the man. When they got close to him, they threw out a life preserver. The man grabbed it and they were pulling him in when, in the blink of an eye, he disappeared. Blood appeared in the water and the rescuers were left to assume that a shark had taken him.

On September 20, 1967, Hurricane Beulah devastated much of the area and sank several boats, but thankfully they were all docked. According to the San Benito News, "A Port Isabel shrimper fleet owner said he lost several boats with loss estimated at $150,000."

The hurricane with its eighteen-to-twenty-foot storm surge made thirty-one cuts through the island, spawned tornadoes and dropped torrential rains, over two feet, in the Rio Grande Valley.

Eunice Varnam suffered a back injury when a boom fell on him. His doctor later told him the strong muscles up and down his back kept him for breaking his spine. Eunice had heard too many stories of men who did suffer broken backs.

On a dark night, the back deck of a working boat is lit up like a stage. It's impossible to see anything off the deck. Nearby, a small boat had not turned on its running lights. Lanny Varnam was working on the back deck when he heard a noise. He described watching in 'slow motion' as their outrigging peeled the top off of the smaller boat.

Mike Zimmerman spoke of a horrific accident that happened while he was in high school. David Lopez's death greatly affected his fellow students as well as the entire Port Isabel community.

David was working on board the *Louisiana Lady* that fished out of the Twin City Co-op. Though David was small, only about five-foot four-inches tall, he was an experienced shrimper, as experienced as a sixteen-year-old can be. He was a handsome boy with long wavy blond hair and blue sky eyes. The boat was making its maiden voyage. She had never fished before. David and the captain were trying her out to see how she worked.

Accidents on board shrimp boats can happen in the blink of an eye. They were picking up the nets after a drag. Although no one witnessed it, the story is that one of David's hands got caught in between the two steel bridle cables. He was guiding cable back and forth as it spun back in, so that it could coil evenly on the large winch spool. A rig man used his hands to guide the cable forward and then back. This is how he made sure the wire would coil in evenly and not bunch up on the cylinder drum.

David Lopez

David was a child of the sixties and seventies. It was also said that perhaps his long hair became entangled in the cables. Regardless of what the winch grabbed first, he was unable to pull his hand and his hair back out after it got caught. The grip of the joined bridles was too tight. The squeeze of these cables powered by monster winches is stronger than any man.

After prolonged wear and tear, masses of tiny rusted needle-sharp bits of cable began to snap off the main strand of wire. These protruding, bristled barbs embedded themselves into his hands.

The loud roar of the big diesel engine and noisy clashing of heavy iron and steel drowned out David's panicked yells for help. By the time the captain heard a faint cry, it was too late. The reeling winch and cables had already swallowed up David. The unyielding force of the winch mangled him.

Horrified at what had happened to David, the captain turned the winch off and hit the brakes. He had to reverse the rotation of the winch drum to loosen and untangle the boy's lifeless body. Like so many other young men before him, David's desire in life was to become a shrimper—a header, a rig man, a captain. Fate and tragedy kept him from reaching his ultimate goal. He became a header. He also became a rig man. An unfortunate accident in one of the most dangerous jobs on earth prevented him from one day becoming a captain.

Every shrimper death at sea is tragic. David's death however hit the community especially hard. He was a teen-aged boy who had not yet begun to live his life. His mother, father and siblings remained in a confused state of shock for a long time. David's peers mourned his death for days in shocked disbelief. The community asked the unanswerable question, "Why did someone so young, so full of life have die so young?" In a vain and fruitless attempt to console the mourners at the memorial service, the priest said "It was God's will." But it was not God's will that he died like he did.

Later, when Mike was away at college, an explosion occurred in his family's shipyard. Lolo Zapata, a welder, was working on a boat. The story is that paint fumes were sealed tight in one of the fuel tanks. When his torch cut through the tank making contact with the fumes, it immediately ignited causing the deadly explosion and killing an employee.

Uvaldo Alaniz's Narrow Escape

Uvaldo's most memorable experience during his shrimping days was almost fatal. He was moments away from death. He was working on a single-rig boat fishing off Port Aransas when a strong norther blew in. They brought the rigging in and as he was securing it to the side railing of the boat, a big wave came over the side hitting them with such force that it ripped loose one of the net doors. The door flew at him, hitting him sideways and knocking him over board. The boats back then had low railings only about knee high. As soon as he hit the water one of the rough waves crashed over him pulling him under the surface. He immediately began to frantically reach for the surface with his hands and arms while kicking his legs against the downward pull of the wave. Feeling that he was still sinking, he kicked off his rubber boots that were full of water and weighing him down. After what seemed like minutes of fighting the strong undertow of the storm, he finally broke the surface frightened, dazed and disoriented. The white caps were breaking over him, slapping viciously from all sides.

His vision was impaired. He couldn't see! The hyper-sea-salt burned and scratched his eyes. Heaving, coughing, gagging, he desperately tried to empty a bloated stomach full of choking Gulf water he had swallowed during the struggle to make it back above water.

Rubbing his eyes and face, he wiped at the stinging spray. He still had water in his stomach. It continued coming up, singeing his throat and vocal cords. He tried yelling. But the only sound that came from his blazing larynx was a mute grunt.

Scared, thinking the worst, Uvaldo kept trying to regain his senses. He took off his trousers. He felt they were making him heavy in the water, with his head bobbing barely above the surface. The captain had turned around and was heading back to the area where he thought Uvaldo had fallen over board. He had one hand on the wheel. The other hand grabbed the handle of the spotlight sitting on top of the wheelhouse. He scoured the surface of the churning water hoping to catch sight of him. In-between sweeping strobes, he hung the guide ropes on the wheel keeping the boat going straight ahead towards the spot where Uvaldo fell. He yelled over the radio that he had a man over board. He changed channels and continued letting everyone within hearing distance know what had happened. He gave his location coordinates, asking for help.

The rig man was outside by the prow following the search light and yelling Uvaldo's name at the top of his lungs hoping to see or hear him yell back. He held a life line in his hands ready to toss it to his mate.

The boat circled around and came right back to where Uvaldo, was in the water. The waves however were too big and somehow they came right up on him without seeing him. Realizing that he was about to be run over, Uvaldo dove back under water. He knew the propeller was going to chop him to pieces. He pointed his nose straight down flinging and stroking his arms as fast as he could. Within seconds, he heard the motor and felt the rotating thrust of the propeller hurling water on him. It missed him by inches!

He came up more frightened than ever. He saw his boat moving away from him. By now he had gotten his voice back. He started screaming but the captain and the other crew member were at the front of the boat. The roar of the wind, the splashing of the waves and the loud rumble of the boat engine muffled his yells. They couldn't hear him.

As Uvaldo drifted further and further away, he saw two other spotlights heading towards him. They were two boats responding to his captain's distress call. One boat was to the right of him. The other to the left. Adrenaline gave him the determination to hold on. As they got closer and closer, the spotlights scanned the water left and right. He yelled and waved his arms. The wake pushed him up, then pulled him back down. They still didn't see him! His rescuers were going to go past him again.

Uvaldo started swimming towards one of the boats hoping to get close enough for them to see him. The closest boat came within arm's length as it passed. As the stern came parallel to him, he saw a net dangling from one of the outriggers above him. He reached for it with one hand—digging his fingers into the mesh. Then he grabbed with his other hand.

The boat continued moving forward. Uvaldo flew in and out of the water like a rag doll flapping in the wind. He banged against the side of the boat as it rolled with the waves. By now he was crying and yelling. Finally, a crew member from the boat running next to them saw Uvaldo being knocked up and down and every which way. He ran to the wheelhouse and alerted his captain.

The captain thrust the throttle into idle and radioed Uvaldo's captain. The crew ran back to the stern to pull the exhausted on deck. As the boat stalled, the net sank in the water. Both Uvaldo and the net were now below the surface. By this time, exhaustion took its toll. His stomach filled with water. His fingers clinched and embedded within the net meshing, Uvaldo was dying.

Realizing that Uvaldo wasn't coming up, the captain ran to the winch and started it. He yelled for a crew member to bring the line to the outrigger over to him. Wrapping the rope around the turning winch head, he saw the rigging begin to rise. When the net cleared the side of the boat, they saw Uvaldo hanging lifeless in the net. They brought him on deck, frantically prying his tangled fingers from the net and laying him flat on the deck.

He looked dead.

In those days CPR training was virtually non-existent among shrimpers. The captain shook him from the shoulders hoping to get a response. He pushed down on his stomach. No response. They continued pushing on his stomach and calling to him, but still no sign of life. As they continued their resuscitation efforts, they pleaded with him to come back from the dead. Suddenly Uvaldo spit up foamy water. A sign of life! Finally sea water spewed up and out of his bloated belly. They turned him on his side and pounded his back to help empty as much water as they could. Uvaldo moaned in pain. He had returned to life.

They sat him up and began to clap their hands. They raised their voices to thank God for sparing Uvaldo from being another fatal statistic to the Gulf of Mexico. The sight of his brother lying there, most likely dead, threw Sandalio Sr. into shock. Uvaldo would remember none of it, although heard the story many times.

He had spent three horrific hours in the water. He remained in shock until after they brought him home. They took him to Doc Hockaday who examined him and told Uvaldo and his family that he was going to be all right. He spent the next few weeks resting and recovering. A month later, he had overcome his fright and was ready to go back out to sea.

The fear may have receded but the memory has stayed with him a lifetime. One can almost see him reliving it as he tells the story.

38

EL CRISTO
DE LOS PESCADORES

Father! Receive the souls of these brave fishermen
Who have sailed through this pass and never returned.

A STATUE, EL CRISTO DE los Pescadores or Christ of
the Fishermen, stands tall in Isla Blanca Park facing the
jetties and the Gulf of Mexico, donated to the Browns-
ville-Port Isabel Shrimp Producers Association by the

De la Lastra Family in memory of Gustavo De la Lastra and Jose Edwardo De la Lastra who lost their lives at sea in 1988. Today the memorial stands as a symbol of hope, faith and safe voyage to all mariners who pass the Brazos de Santiago Pass on their way out to sea. It also welcomes all sailors and boaters returning home. Huge granite rocks form the base, with plaques honoring area fisherman who lost their lives at sea. If you visit the statue, you will find flowers left at the plaques.

The statue elicits emotional responses—sorrow for the ones who lost their lives, hope for those who still sail beyond the shores of Brazos de Santiago Pass and peace that Christ watches over them.

The names of the fishermen on the plaques are listed here. Each man who failed to return from the sea left his mark on Brownsville/Port Isabel and in the hearts of the family members who mourn him. The plaques include the fisherman's name, the boat he was on and the date of his death. They are listed here in alphabetical order.

Bartolo Arellano, the *Melody*, November 23, 196?

Javier "El Capi" Balandran, the *Little Stevie*, August 14, 1987

Ricardo A. Bella, the *Colombia*, June 11, 1950

John Richard Card, Sr., the *Lady of the Sea*, February 29, 1960

Carlos "Boy" Casanova, the *Inshala*, January 10, 1973

Abelardo Castillo, the *Republic*, November 5, 1960

Gregorio Castillo, the *Tide II*, November 19, 1970

Isaac C. Cervantes, the *Albatross*, August 14, 1991

Gustavo De la Lastra, the *Wilderness*, July 7, 1988

Jose Eduardo De la Lastra, the *Wilderness*, July 7, 1988

Eduardo "Chapo" Esquitin, the *Apache Brave*, December 15, 1977

John Louis Farroba, the *Portegui*, March 23, 1978

Adolfo Gonzalez, the *Louisiana Lady*, April 14, 1991

Robert "Pink Panther" Hauring, the *Maria Elena*, June 23, 2010

Arturo "Turi" Hernandez, the *Mario Arturo II*, December 15, 2010

David Lopez, Jr., the *Louisiana Lady*, February 7, 1972

James "Jimmy" Roy Melina, the *Lori Dawn VI*, August 11, 2002

Leo Norman, the *Prawn Queen*, August 17, 1952

Refugio Ochoa, the *Miss Monica*, September 7, 1968

Juan G. Rivera, the *Aquarius Lady*, August 25, 1982

Manuel A. "The Judge" Rodriguez, the *Linda C*, January 23, 1963

Refugio "Cuco" Sanchez, the *Lady Brenda*, December 9, 1978

Jose Angel Torres, the *Dewey*, December 3, 1963

Jesus Vasquez, the *Esto King*, May 15, 1985

Benito Villagran, the *Lucilla Ann*, November 28, 2000

39

FAMILY LIFE

> You gotta be a little weird to stay away from home that long.
> Charles Burnell

L: Vicki Gonzalez R: Darlene Lacoste
Texas Shrimp Association Convention 2018

DURING THE SHRIMPING SEASON, only wives and children occupied Port Isabel homes. While the men spent months at sea, the responsibility for home and childcare fell to the wives. They managed household money and developed their own household systems.

The men we interviewed were generous with praise for "a job well done."

There stories were similar. On their return from sea, the men collected their money, paid off any commissary debts—and took the remainder home for their families. They also brought their families fresh shrimp.

Almost all of the interviewees spoke of celebratory reunion dinners out. Mares Martinez always took his family to Vermillion in Brownsville.

Missing important family functions and happenings is a way of life for shrimpers. They understand this when they decide to make shrimping their livelihood. They are often out fishing during children's birthdays, ballgames and dance recitals. They know they will not be home for much of the year. Most of them grew up as sons of shrimpers themselves. They remember what it was like to grow up with an absent father. They all missed their dads when they were gone for many days and nights at a time. Yet knowing that feeling didn't stop many young boys in Port Isabel from yearning to become shrimpers themselves. Perhaps because they are sons of shrimpers, they were born with shrimping blood flowing through their veins. Perhaps it was the larger than life persona and aura that emanates from mariners.

Mares Martinez and his wife Josefina had nine children—five girls and four boys. Josefina kept a notebook for each child. In it she listed their accomplishments, their problems and their behavior. When Mares returned home, he could then catch up on each one. Today his children are his pride and joy and he credits Josefina with their success.

One time the boat owner, Sammy Snodgrass, asked Mares why he never cashed his checks. Surprised, he had no answer. That was when he found out Josefina had saved more than enough to make a down payment on his first boat. She encouraged him to buy land in town. He did and sold it at a profit.

Mares remembers Josefina with affection and pride, having lost her after sixty-two years of marriage.

Charles Burnell takes pride in having his son, daughter and daughter-in-law work with him. He praised his ex-wife for raising them and taking care of the home front while he was away. He spoke of the difficulty of long separations. Once when his wife asked him if he thought of her when he was away, she was appalled at his answer. "I don't have time to think about you. I have to focus every minute on the job at hand."

Other shrimpers echoed his response. Several spoke of the intense concentration required to avoid accidents, bring in the nets and take care of the boat. They described shrimping as "a twenty-four seven" job. When they're not working, they are sleeping.

Mike Cateora was a third-generation shrimper. Born and raised in Port Isabel, he knew no other life growing up. He didn't see his childhood as being different from most of his friends. Almost everyone in town was connected to shrimping. Mike's father was a boat and fish house owner. His grandfather was too. After the deaths of his grandfather and father, Mike kept the business going.

The Varnam siblings agreed that life was better when their dad was home. They looked forward to spending time with him and their mother together.

Billy Holland was a lifelong shrimper and independent boat owner. Independent boat owners were individuals who owned and captained their own boat. They did not belong to a company fleet of boats. A company fleet may be six or more boats.

Billy admitted that the many days away from his wife and kids was difficult. His family however accepted the shrimping lifestyle without question. He thinks his wife did a marvelous job. It wasn't easy for her and he appreciated how hard it must have been to be the sole parent for seven months each year. "She'd cover some for the girls, but she told me everything about the boys. I always had a talk with them about their behavior." He didn't want them to become shrimpers like him and he's glad they listened to him.

Jasper Bodden, another long-time shrimper and one of the few remaining shrimp boat companies still operating of out of Port Isabel said his wife had no problems with their lifestyle. Both he and his wife appreciate the fact that shrimping gave their family a good life.

Sandalio Alaniz admitted that at times his family's social lives affected his life at sea. If one of his children had an important event that he would miss, he found it difficult to focus on his work. Knowing he would see his kids off for the first day of their new school year was hard. Missing school performance programs—especially during their kindergarten and elementary school years—was trying. These are the times when children are tiny, funny and entertaining. He didn't see his children perform their first uncoordinated "Cotton-Eyed Joe" dance or sing their first "God Bless America" in the children's choir.

Sandalio is most appreciative to his one true love, his wife Betty. She managed everything on the home front, while he was working. She took care of all the bills and budgeted the money. She reared and disciplined the children, nursed them and took them to the doctor when they were sick. She dealt with school issues and challenges associated with raising toddlers, then pre-teens, then teen-agers. When Sandalio came home tired and exhausted, after forty or fifty days and nights of fishing, there were no serious disciplinary concerns waiting for him to resolve.

Shrimper wives are constantly under the watchful eyes of the rest of the community. They are judged by how they keep house, manage the kids, take care of the money—and their fidelity to their husbands. Betty Alaniz exemplified all those traits. Not all shrimper wives do.

"We took the families under our wing," Red Sagnes said of his days as manager of the fish house/ freezer, Twin City Co-op. "If they came to us needing money, we made the advance." Household expenses are never ending. Wives, however, were careful about how much advanced money they requested. They didn't want their husband to come back after a long fishing trip and be handed an accounts statement receipt with a small cash net balance. The companies monitored the advances to the wife. They made it a point to communicate any advance payment with the crew.

Linda Sagnes, in her work as home visitor/school community liaison with Port Isabel High School, did her best to keep children of shrimpers in school. "I would go and knock on their doors and tell them to get to school." Children of shrimpers are eligible for college scholarships and financial assistance if they finished school. They must first fill out and complete a Texas Education Agency Migrant eligibility form. If they meet the eligibility criteria qualifying them as migrants, they may apply for college financial assistance.

Like children of farm worker families who migrate throughout Texas and other agricultural-focused states throughout the United States, shrimper families may a qualify for Texas Education Agency benefits. The money, sent to states that have agriculture and aquaculture working families, comes from the U.S. Department of Education at the federal level. The name of the college financial assistance that helps migrant children pay their college tuition is called "The College Assistance Migrant Program" or "CAMP."

Rudy Garcia, co-author of this work, worked alongside Linda Sagnes and Mr. Frank Mata, Assistant Superintendent of Schools, Point Isabel ISD to recruit and implement the migrant program in Port Isabel. Many Port Isabel High School graduates, who were children of shrimpers and shrimping related industries or aquaculture benefited from the College Assistance Migrant Program, to fund their college education.

The advent of the cell phone greatly improved family communication. Men at sea can call home for birthdays, holidays and other special events. Wives are also able to contact their husbands when necessary. Often times however the boats are so far out at sea that they are out of cell phone range. When this happens, captains resort back to the always reliable radio to make contact with the family.

Were there ever problems? Sure. Most of the men spoke of shrimpers who drank away their earnings or whose marriages broke up. Like all industries, it depended on the personalities, morals and behavior of those involved.

40

STORIES AT SEA

WHEN THE INTERNATIONAL WATERS restricted only twelve miles off a country's shore, Gulf fishermen enjoyed the benefits of the full Gulf waters. They were able to fish virtually year-round. Shrimp were plentiful up and down the coast. During the winter months, when shrimp sought warmer waters, American shrimpers followed and spent the winter months fishing Mexican waters.

The Bay of Campeche was a favorite spot. Fishing was easy. Shrimp were plentiful. Fishing companies sent their boats to Campeche because shrimp boats at that time were mostly ice boats. Boats with ice were dispatched to fetch the catch and return with their bins filled to capacity while other vessels continued fishing nonstop.

During these months locals always knew when a shrimp boat was going south to fish Campeche. The tell-tale sign was the groceries. Shrimpers would fill shopping cart after shopping cart, overflowing with groceries for the long haul.

Local grocers loved it. They made tons of money as did the ice houses, fuel companies, and the entire community. The Mexicans also enjoyed the money that flowed into their local economy during the winter months. After working hard offshore for weeks at time, captains would reward their crew by going ashore for two or three days of hard-earned R&R. Imagine if you will, dozens of shrimpers with dollars in their pockets coming into port for a fun time. However, some shrimper stories are best left there in all those ports of call.

It was a good and profitable business arrangement for both countries that lasted many years. Then as bureaucrats, almost always do, they decided to meddle. As a result, both the U.S. and Mexico extended their international boundaries to 200 miles. The prime winter fishing grounds were no longer available to U.S. shrimpers.

Many captains and shrimping companies didn't take kindly to the new law. Some customs and traditions are difficult to change. Because they were accustomed to fishing these now forbidden waters, some captains decided they would still fish their traditional fishing grounds. They continued to head down south, except now they were fishing illegally. Both governments held them accountable to the new law. The U.S. Government, as well as the Mexican government, prosecuted them. For a while, many got away with it, but as the Mexican Navy gun boats became more familiar with the fishing grounds the American captains frequented, they grew better at patrolling. The number of captains being caught increased. They paid fines and/or bribes because the fishing was still profitable. In some cases, it was common for captains to take one or two suitcases each filled with $5,000. If they were caught and taken to Tampico, they paid off the guards. As time passed, the Mexican officials decided that the bribe money was not enough. The money was considered a bonus. They decided they were going to take the money, confiscate the boat, the shrimp, the entire gear, and equipment. The crew ended up in jail while hefty fines and more bribes were imposed. It gradually put an end to the American shrimper fishing south of the border.

Fishing in Mexican waters was a common risk taken by many Texas and Louisiana shrimpers. During the first weeks of every new shrimp season, there are plenty of shrimp for shrimpers to harvest in Texas and U.S. waters. There is no need for shrimpers to sail south into Mexican waters to fish.

Shrimp is a migratory species and shrimpers know their movement patterns. So during cold winter months when the shrimp become scarce north of the Rio Grande, some shrimpers risk it all and venture during the cover of night into Mexican waters. They dare to risk it all because they have bills to pay and families to support. There illegal fishing in Mexican waters is like a cat and mouse game. The shrimpers leave the safety, protection and jurisdiction of the U.S. Government (Coast Guard) and enter another country's territory to harvest shrimp in their waters.

Most shrimpers stay close to the U.S. water boundary while fishing in Mexican waters. They do this because they are well aware that the Mexican Navy gun boats are patrolling the eastern perimeter of their jurisdictional waters. If they are picked up on radar by a Mexican Navy gun boat, and in most cases they are, they are able to pick up their nets and head back to American waters. This is when the chase begins.

Prior to the chase however both captains and their first mates keep a constant eye on their radar screens. The first bleeping dot that appears on the shrimper's screen, moving fast towards them from the west means the gun boat has picked them up on their screen. It's time to run. The chase is on. The shrimper captain yells out the alarm. The crew immediately spring into action. Time to pick up the nets and pick them up fast. The Mexican Navy gun boat is a lot bigger and a whole lot faster than the shrimp boat. Although the shrimp boat is trawling in the dark with all lights off to avoid been seen, it really doesn't matter. The gun boats have them locked in on radar.

The main reason the shrimper keeps his lights off is safety. The gun boat will not hesitate to fire on the shrimpers if they can see them. Fishing in Mexican waters is not an act of war by any means. Nor is the Mexican gun boat under any threat by the shrimpers. They both understand this. It is just an illegal act and the gun boat captain's duty is to enforce the sovereignty of their waters. Once the Mexican captain has the shrimper in his sight, he keeps the spot lights on the boat and sirens blasting. He calls on the radio and bull horn for the shrimper to surrender.

He is told that he is fishing in Mexican waters and is under arrest. He should bring his shrimp boat to an idle stop and wait to be detained. All shrimpers make a run for it hoping to escape back to the US.

Some shrimpers venture too far into Mexican waters and simply cannot outrun the gun boat. During the chase when the captain refuses to heed the call of capture, the Mexican gun boat captain will give the order to fire warning shots in front of the shrimp boat's prow. This usually works and the shrimper will cease his escape efforts. There have been reported incidents of the Mexican gun boat actually bumping the shrimp boats to make them stop. Once captured, the captain immediately gets on his radio and lets it be known that he, his boat, and his crew are being detained by the Mexican gun boat. He gives out his name as well as the name of his shrimp boat and what fishing company he works for.

Within a matter of minutes, the entire Texas shrimping fleet is aware of what happened. In most cases the shrimp boat owner is not aware his boat is fishing in Mexican waters. In fact, most boat owners strictly forbid their captains to fish there. The risk is too costly and the possibility of losing the boat is real. It may be kept in litigation within the Mexican court system for months. The captain and crew will be arrested, interrogated, and thrown in jail but in most cases the crew will be released a few days after paying the fines. The Mexican government realizes that the crew has no authority on the boat. They are under the command of the captain who made the decision to fish in Mexican waters. In the captain's case his fine is substantially higher than his crew. He is the violator and sole responsible person for committing the crime of fishing illegally. The big loser is the boat owner. His boat is impounded and held until litigations resolved and the hefty fine paid. There are cases where the boat owner simply does not have or cannot put together the money to pay the fine on his boat. When this happens the Mexican government keeps the boat and makes it part of their shrimping fleet.

As soon as the boat is moored into a Mexican port, usually Tampico for Texas shrimpers, Mexican dock workers board the vessel and unload the shrimp. Other workers strip the equipment on the boat, taking cables, winches, nets, ropes, chains, doors, radios, radars, and fuel. Everything is taken. At that point the boat becomes property of the Mexican government. The only thing left with the boat is the engine.

Word of the boat's seizure by the Mexican Navy reaches the boat owner almost immediately. As soon as the capture hits the air waves, he hears the bad news. Plans to get his boat back starts right away. He makes phone calls to the crew's families. The U.S. Coast Guard is contacted to get any information they may have regarding the seizure. For the most part the Coast Guard is usually aware of the situation. There is not much they can do as far as negotiating with the Mexican government for the return of the shrimp boat to its owners. They do make a report of any information they may have based on their radar monitoring. The owners contact their lawyers. Lawyers contact State and Federal officials, such as Congressman and Representatives and Consulates. Travel permits to travel into Mexico are obtained by the boat owner and attorney.

They go and meet with Mexican government officials to request permission to visit with the jailed crew, who have by this time gone before a Mexican Federal Judge, and been charged with the crime of violating Mexican territorial waters law. They are then given permission to go see their boat but not allowed to board it.

After this the negotiations begin. First, the release of the crew. The fine is set. In Mexico, a money amount always starts high. This happens with every transaction whenever money is involved. That's the way they do business.

The crew is released once their fine is settled. Next, the negotiation for cost of the fine and conditions set for the release of the boat. This is what gets expensive. It runs into the thousands of dollars.

Mexican officials know that the shrimp boat owner will pay the agreed fine to get their boat back as long as it doesn't bankrupt him.

Stories abound of shrimpers caught in or near Mexican waters.

Firpo Tower, a feisty old shrimp boat owner, had three of his boats fishing in Mexico, off the Tampico coast. They were in Mexican waters and the Mexican Navy seized the boats. They confiscated the shrimp. Firpo, determined to get his boats back, went down to Tampico. He was accompanied by one of his other brave captains. Early one morning they left their hotel room without checking out. They took with them two compasses they had brought with them. They went to a waterfront cantina that had outside tables across the street from the dock where his boats were tied up. They ordered two cervezas and two breakfast tacos.

There they waited for the right moment. When the Mexicans guarding the boats left their posts and went to a neighboring cantina to drink coffee and eat their breakfast, they sprang into action. Firpo dropped a fifty-peso bill on the table and they walked briskly to his boats. Fortunately for Firpo, his boats were tied up next to each other. No other boats were tied up next to him starboard side. In an instant, they quickly cut the ropes. Firpo cut the prow rope. His captain cut the stern rope. Firpo dashed to the wheelhouse and started the engine of the port side boat. He turned the wheel to the right as far as it could turn. He then jumped out on the starboard side and cut the other prow rope. He side hurtled across the railing and into the wheelhouse of the next boat. His captain was cutting the stern rope tethering them together. Firpo started the other engine and again spun the wheel of that boat to the right as far as it would go.

By this time his captain was behind the wheel of his boat. Firpo shouted to his captain, "Vamonos." In one synchronized motion, they pushed the throttle full speed ahead. They were off! Taking their lives in their hands and hoping for the best. They steered north-northeast as fast as the boats could go. They did not know how much fuel they had in their tanks. They hoped they had enough to make it into international waters. Once they got there, they would call the U. S. Coast Guard for assistance. By the time, the Mexican guards finished drinking coffee and having breakfast and walked back across the street to their assigned post. Firpo, his captain, and his boats were out in the open sea speeding east-northeast.

A frantic call by the Mexican Navy went out. Two fugitive American pirates had highjacked two confiscated shrimp boats. Not knowing exactly where they were the Mexican Navy sent out their gun boats in search of the pirates as they called them. The order was to fine them and bring them back to Tampico. Shoot at will when you see them.

The Mexican Navy eventually spotted Firpo and his captain with the two boats, traveling northeast, the boats were sitting light in the water. The only weight they were carrying was the fuel in the tanks. Even with that, Firpo and his captain didn't know how much fuel they had. They cut through swelled wave after swelled wave. They came out its back side, flying in midair before landing directly on the next wave's face, splitting that one open too. The gun boats could see the white-water spray splash high and wide on either side of the boats.

The Mexican Navy continued giving chase hoping to overtake them. The two Firpo boats were rapidly approaching U.S. Waters—and they were running out of time and Mexican water space. They were not going to be able to capture them.

In a last-ditch effort to make the two escaping boats cease and surrender, the gun boat captain gave the order to fire on them. They fired several rounds. Firpo was not about to stop now. He was determined and his mind was locked on getting back to his home port with his two boats. As far as he was concerned it had now become a life or death situation. There was no way he was going to allow himself or his captain to be taken prisoners by the Mexicans. He knew that if they were taken back to Mexico to be tried for piracy, in front of a Mexican judge and jury, they would spend the rest of their adult lives in a Mexican jail. It would take years and every penny he had to get him out of jail. The Mexicans kept firing. They did not aim directly at the boats. They fired in front of them and overhead. The last thing the Mexican Navy wanted was to create an international incident with the United

States. However, the life threatening gamble paid off for Firpo and his captain. They made it back with two of his boats. He had lost the boat he left behind. The Mexican government kept it.

Firpo got some satisfaction. In time he made up the loss of his boat. The Mexican Navy, however to this day, still lives with the embarrassment that an American shrimp boat owner and one of his captains took back two captured boats right from under their noses and made it back to Port Isabel. The Mexican Navy called them pirates. Port Isabel and the shrimping family called them heroes.

Red Sagnes told the story of a friend who was fishing off Tampico. One of the crew, the header, was tired. He felt he had already been out at sea for too many days and wanted to come home. When the header told the captain he was ready to come home, of course the captain refused. A crew member does not give the captain orders. It's the other way around.

However, a captain must be careful of his crew members whenever they began to show signs of emotional and physical breakdown. An unstable crew member can become dangerous to himself as well as to the rest of the crew. It's known that some crew members who have wanted to come home have actually jumped overboard in desperation. Some have sabotaged an engine break down or caused injury to themselves to force the captain to come back to port.

In most cases a captain will use his experience and better judgment to rid himself of an emotionally broken crew member. Depending in the person's mental state, the captain will determine where and when to take him in to Port. If the disturbed or fatigued member is stable enough to be taken to the nearest port away from home, the captain will take him there and give him enough money to buy bus fare back home. If his mental and physical state is grave, the captain will keep him on board guarded. He will let the Coast Guard know of the situation. An assessment is made and if the Coast Guard needs to send a helicopter to boat lift the crew member, they will. Otherwise, the crew member will remain guarded on board until they get back home.

In this case, the captain drove the boat up onto Monkey Island and threw the header off the boat, telling him to get home the best way he could. The guy made it home and later showed up to collect his pay.

One thing is certain of any crew member who has being out fishing. They will always know when the accounts of the shrimp cargo are being settled. They will be there on the dock where the boat is tied up no matter what condition they are in to collect their pay.

Captain Carlos Medina was working for the Zimmerman Brothers. The Mexican Navy patrolling their waters caught him fishing in their territory. Captain Carlos made a run for it. He tried to make it back across into U.S. waters but was unable to outrun the bigger, faster Mexican gun boat. During the pursuit and after several warning shots in front of his prow, Carlos still refused to surrender. The captain of the gun boat decided to ram the rear of Medina's boat, disabling his rudder. Unable to steer his vessel. Captain Carlos had no choice but to give himself up. They took possession of the boat and towed it to Tampico, where they confiscated the entire catch as well, as all of the supplies and equipment. The Zimmerman Brothers had to jump through many hoops and pay a lot of money in fines to get their boat back. Captain Carlos' refusal to stop when they came on him also cost him dearly. He was kept prisoner in a Tampico jail for twenty-nine days and had to pay a big fine. Carlos claims he didn't want to stop because he was certain he was not fishing in Mexican waters. He was close to Mexico but not in Mexico. The Mexican Navy of course say he was. Oftentimes when a shrimp boat was captured by the Mexican gunboat, the two stories never coincided. The shrimper said he was not in Mexican waters and the Mexicans say he was. So who do you believe? In the end it didn't matter. Mexico had the boat and the only way to get it back was to pay. The U.S. Government was of little help to shrimpers during these situations. They sometimes sent the U.S. Consul in Mexico to talk to the Mexican officials, but the talks were merely a formality. The seized boat remained under Mexican control and was not released until its owner, no matter what the U.S. Government said, met all demands for fines.

Red Sagnes remembered another time when a shrimper couldn't pay for his boats. He had several

—some new and some junk. Red watched as the lender had the boats sawed up in the water and salvaged.

Several years ago, I met a former Port Isabel captain Rocky (Frank Paprocki), who was believed to have shot his crew. He fled to Cuba where he was jailed by the Castro dictatorship. Sometime after his release, he returned to the area.

Rocky was the captain of the *Esto Fleet* which was owned by Walter and Frances Rull. There are many versions of what, how and why the killings happened on or about November, 19, 1967. During the off season, Rocky and his crew were fishing in Texas waters down on the Bay of Campeche. Many other Texas boats were fishing there too. Captain Rocky and his crew were anchored in the swallows as they called waters off the beach from Ciudad Carmen. They were tied up and anchored port side to starboard with the older shrimping vessel, the *Miss Sondra Leigh*.

That night, the two crews had been drinking. Eventually, an argument began, as was a common occurrence with drunk shrimpers. The disagreement was over money. Rocky's rig man, a guy by the name of Billy Joe Pool, wanted a money advance on his share of the shrimp they had on board.

Author's Note: Asking for and receiving money advances is a common part of the earning settlement for shrimpers. The advance payment is almost always given at the captain's discretion. The procedure begins with the captain radioing the boat owner how much shrimp they have caught. The boat owner then calculates an estimate on the value of the catch. Depending on how much they have, the owner figures out if—and how much of—an advance payment is merited. The money goes to the shrimper's wife or the shrimper's parent if the shrimper is not married. Advances sustain the family financially until the boat returns to port with their final catch total.

After all the shrimp is processed and sold, the boat owner deducts expenses. The boat and crew share the profits. The crew's share is further divided between the captain and the rig man with the captain getting the bigger share, of course. The captain and rig man then pays the header with each contributing the same amount. At this point, advances are deducted from the final pay settlement.

Eventually, the argument on the *Esto Fleet* and the *Miss Sondra Leigh* turned into an all-out brawl. After the brawl, Rocky went to his captain's bunk to get away from the melee. His crew stayed out on the deck of the *Miss Sondra Leigh* and continued drinking.

The next day after everyone slept off the stupor from the night before, Billy Joe Pool approached Rocky again asking for the advance. His wife was going to go to the fish house the next day to ask the boat owner for the money. Rocky, who was hung over and in a bad mood again, refused Billy Joe the advance. The header, an unidentified Mexican national, also requested an advance. Rocky refused him too.

Rocky told them they needed to wait a few more days. He planned on sending their load back to Port Isabel later that same day. He had already made an arrangement with two other shrimp boats, the *June* and the *Sailfish*, to transport the shrimp back to the fish house. The *June* and the *Sailfish* had already completed their trip and were heading back to home to Port Isabel.

In those days, all of the shrimp boats were ice boats. The longest they could keep the shrimp iced down and fresh was about twenty days. They had already been in Campeche for about ten to twelve days. All fish houses had an agreement to transport each other's shrimp back to home port whenever boats finished their trip. It was the only way they could preserve their catch and prevent spoilage. Rocky told his crew that when the shrimp was unloaded and processed back in Port Isabel, they could get their advance. Needless to say his crew were not happy with this decision.

Regardless, as Rocky told them, the shrimp was loaded on the *June* and the *Sailfish* and shipped back to Port Isabel. Rocky radioed boat owner Walter Rull how much shrimp would be there in a few days. He could then give the wives the advance money.

Also, coming back with the shrimp from the *Esto Fleet* and the *Miss Sondra Leigh* was *Miss Sondra Leigh* crew member Richard Lymon. Lymon had become an uncooperative worker. He didn't want to work anymore so Captain Tyndall sent him back with the *June*. As it turned out, Lymon's unwillingness to work saved his life.

After the *June* and the *Sailfish* sailed for Port Isabel, the *Esto Fleet* and the *Miss Sandra Leigh* stayed tied up and anchored together—and the drinking resumed. Some beers later, the argument about the refused money advance began again. There were still bad feelings about Rocky's decision to change the procedure.

To make matter worse, Rocky and Captain Tyndall also got into an argument—but it wasn't over money. Well, maybe it was. They disagreed as to the amount of shrimp each of their boats sent back. Each captain felt cheated out of some of the shrimp. And shrimp equals money. The entire matter escalated. Rocky's crew was against him. Captain Tyndall and his crew were against him as well.

Rocky became enraged! He left the *Miss Sondra Leigh* and went aboard his boat, the *Esto Fleet*. The crews of both boats remained on the *Miss Sondra Leigh*. The captains yelled obscenities at each other across the bow of their respective boats. The mood was bad and getting worse. The rig man for the *Miss Sondra Leigh*, a fellow by the name of Louis Duhon, decided he didn't want to stick around and listen to the two angry captains exchanging insults. To get away from the fracas, he went down in the ice bins of the "hole" of the boat to do some work.

A short while later, he heard gun shots. Within moments, he heard two more. He poked his head out of the hole. The Mexican National was lying dead on deck. Duhon looked towards the cabin and saw Captain Tyndall being shot dead too. Rocky had come back from the *Esto Fleet* with his .357 Magnum and was shooting everyone.

Fearing for his own life, Duhon hurried back down into the hole and grabbed a life jacket. Then he cautiously poked his head out of the hole and looked around. Gun in hand, Rocky was searching the boat for the rest of the crew. Duhon had little time to save himself.

With no safe place left on board the *Miss Sondra Leigh*, Duhon bolted out of the hole and jumped overboard. As he swam towards the beach at Ciudad Carmen, he heard more shots.

Louis Duhon, swam faster! Rocky had gone mad. He was going to kill them all!

After counting the dead bodies, Rocky realized that something was wrong. There were three dead men—Captain Tyndall of the *Miss Sondra Leigh*, Billy Joe Pool, rig man for the *Esto Fleet*—and Rocky's Mexican header. There should have been be four. Duhon. Where was the *Miss Sondra Leigh* rig man?

Rocky went to the back deck and saw the hole lid open. He peered into the hole. No Duhon. He went down to the to the engine room. He didn't find the rig man there either. Back up on deck, he realized Duhon was not on board the *Miss Sondra Leigh*. Rocky jumped over to the *Esto Fleet*. Duhon was nowhere on board of either boat. He scanned the surface of the water around both boats. And then he spotted Duhon, swimming towards shore.

Duhon later said that he heard Rocky yell, "you're next" and then two shots. At first, Duhon reported that he had been wounded by one of those shots. He also described drifting and swimming for two days in the Bay of Campeche, trying to make it to shore. The strong currents kept him pushing him back until a Mexican fishing boat came across him and took him on board, dropping him off closer to shore. Mexican authorities found him in shock and suffering from exposure. They took him to the hospital in Ciudad Carmen. The medical professionals treated him for exposure and returned him to the Mexican authorities saying they had not found any gunshot wounds on him. The Mexican police threw Duhon in jail and kept him there for days as they continued their part of the investigation.

Based on the information Duhon gave them, the Mexican Navy searched for the *Miss Sondra Leigh*. They found her a couple of days later in the Bay of Campeche, almost totally submerged on her side on top of a reef.

When the Mexican divers went inside the sunken boat, they found two dead men chained up inside. Captain Tyndall's body was in the wheelhouse and Billy Joe Pool was down inside of the hole. The Mexican was not on the *Miss Sondra Leigh*. His body was never recovered.

There was no sign of the *Este Fleet*. The authorities later learned that in the hours after the murders, the two boats remained tied together side by side. Eventually, Rocky picked up anchor and sailed for deeper water with the *Miss Sondra Leigh* in tow.

Another Port Isabel shrimp boat the *Tony Gene*, captained by Oscar Grisham was in the vicinity. Captain Grisham saw the boats motoring out to sea tied side by side.

As is the protocol of the sea, whenever the master of a marine vessel sees another sea vessel in distress or in need of assistance, he is obligated by maritime rule to assist in whichever way he can. Captain Grisham who was familiar with the boats, as well as their captains, did what was expected of him. He got on his radio and called out to both captains. Rocky was the only one to reply back.

"What is the matter," Grisham asked. "And which of the boats is the disabled one?"

Rocky answered back that the *Miss Sondra Leigh* was the one that was disabled. Grisham informed Rocky that he had finished his trip and was returning to Port

Isabel. He would be glad to tow the *Miss Sondra Leigh* back to Port Isabel.

Rocky turned down the offer.

Captain Grisham, suspecting that there was more trouble with the boats than what Rocky reported, made a radio call to the *Miss Sondra Leigh*. He got no response. He repeated his radio call several more times. Still no response from the *Miss Sondra Leigh*.

The side-by-side boats continued out toward deeper water. He decided to get a better look at them. Following at a distance, he made radio contact with Rocky again. He asked for information on the *Miss Sondra Leigh*.

Rocky responded that the *Miss Sondra Leigh* had lost all power including her radio power. Rocky repeated that he didn't need Captain Grisham's help.

Captain Grisham backed down but kept Rocky and his boat in sight. After following Rocky for awhile, he saw the *Miss Sondra Leigh* and the *Esto Fleet* separate. Had the *Miss Sondra Leigh* fixed her mechanical and electrical problems and was now operating under her own power?

Moments later, Grisham saw the *Esto Fleet* make a wide three-hundred-and-sixty-degree maneuver. She picked up speed and headed straight towards the *Miss Sondra Leigh*. He watched in disbelief before radioing Rocky to ask him what he was doing. Rocky didn't respond.

Rocky zeroed his *Esto Fleet* on the *Miss Sondra Leigh* and rammed her "T-bone" style. Debris flew up in the air above the cabin and in all other directions. The *Miss Sondra Leigh* was a wooden boat, the *Esto Fleet* a big new steel hull with a powerful engine. The impact ripped a hole in the side of the *Miss Sondra Leigh* and she began taking on water. Rocky reversed his boat, put it in forward thrust—and rammed her again. The force of the second and final blow pushed the *Miss Sondra Leigh* into a slow sinking drift.

The Miss Sondra Leigh

Rocky turned the *Esto Fleet* around and headed East full throttle.

Captain Grisham put his boat in gear and motored away. He realized Rocky had gone mad and did not want him to come after him and ram his boat too. He reported what he had seen after he got back to Port Isabel on November 21, 1967, two days after the incident. By than it was too late to find Rocky. He had a boat full of fuel and enough food to hide out wherever it was that he went.

The bodies of Billy Joe Pool and Captain Tyndall never made it back to Port Isabel. They were buried somewhere in Mexico. Rocky and the *Esto Fleet* were never found. Some rumors said he was dead, but that was never confirmed.

Rocky made one last radio communication with Walter Rull, the owner of the *Esto Fleet* though. He told him there was no need to give Billy Joe Pool's wife a money advance because Billy Joe was no longer a crew member of the *Esto Fleet*. And then the radio went silent.

When Louis Duhon was released from the Mexican jail, the authorities sent him back to the U.S. He reentered the country through Reynosa, Mexico and McAllen, Texas. He told the FBI what had happened, changing the part of his story about Rocky shooting him. In his FBI interview in McAllen, he told them that Rocky shot at him but missed. Ultimately, Rocky was charged the murder of Billy Joe Pool, Captain Tyndall, and the unknown Mexican header.

After the FBI interrogation, Duhon returned to Port Isabel. A few days later, the FBI came back to ask him some more questions about the incident down in Campeche. Duhon was nowhere to be found.

The murder of three Port Isabel shrimpers and the sinking of the *Miss Sondra Leigh* while fishing for shrimp down in the Bay of Campeche, Mexico on November 19, 1967 became legend. For many years Rocky's fate and the whereabouts of the shrimp boat *June* remained a mystery as well. At least until 1989-90. Twenty-three years later, Rocky reappeared on the shrimping docks of Port Isabel.

Frank "Rocky" Poprocki

The shrimping season was about to begin and Rocky was looking for work on a shrimp boat. He didn't have much luck getting hired. Most of the captains recognized him and remembered what he had done years before. He was just about to run out of boats at the end of the dock. Captain Aaron Moore, owner operator the Trade Way, was preparing his boat for the season. He had two heads but did not yet have a rig man. Rocky asked him for a job and Captain Aaron gave him an impromptu interview on the dock. Captain Aaron, feeling Rocky answered enough of his questions to his satisfaction, decided he was knowledgeable enough about rigging. With the season opening the next day, he needed a rig man. He asked Rocky his name and Rocky said, "Frank Paprocki."

Captain Aaron told him he was hired and that he should go get his gear and come back right away. There was still much work to do on the *Trade Way* before she was ready to ship out.

Rocky went fishing with Captain Aaron, his crew, and the *Trade Way*. Two weeks later, the *Trade Way* and her full crew was back in Port unloading their shrimp. As Rocky and the headers were busy on the *Trade Way*'s back deck, Captain Whitman Bodden, a veteran shrimper, boat owner, and long-time friend of Captain Aaron, came over to where the *Trade Way* was docked. He and Captain Aaron began talking regular shrimp talk. Things like how was your trip? How much shrimp did you catch? The size of the shrimp, the market price of shrimp—and other normal conversations Captains have.

Captain Whitman looked to the back deck of the *Trade Way* and saw a familiar face. He took a longer, closer look. Captain Whitman had been in Port Isabel, for many years, far longer than Captain Aaron. He knew and remembered just about everyone who had fished there. Then he recognized the man. Frank Poprocki. How was it that Rocky could be back in Port Isabel? He pulled Captain Aaron a few steps away from the *Trade Way* out of ear shot from the crew.

"Aaron do you know who that man working on your back deck is?" Captain Whitman asked.

Captain Aaron responded, "Which man?"

"That one. The Anglo one."

"His name is Frank."

"His name may be Frank but that's Rocky," Captain Whitman said. "That's the Rocky who killed his crew and the crew of the *Miss Sondra Leigh* down in Campeche years ago."

"I don't know anything about that. All I know is that I needed a rig man. He seemed to know what he was taking about when I asking him questions about rigging so I hired him. It turns out he does know how to rig on a boat. He did good work. I didn't have any problems with him. He got along well with the rest of the crew too. I will talk to him about what you have just told me though. I don't want to put myself and the crew in any danger."

After Captain Whitman left, Captain Aaron went on board the *Trade Way* and asked Rocky to come to the wheelhouse with him.

Captain Aaron told Rocky what he had just heard from Captain Whitman.

Rocky said he had seen Captain Whitman—and he knew right away that he would recognize him. Rocky told Captain Aaron that what Captain Whitman told him was true. He did kill those shrimpers in Campeche but it happened many years ago. It was in the past. He had paid for his crime. He was a changed man. There was nothing to worry about.

Captain Aaron asked Rocky to tell him what happened and if he was satisfied with the story, he could continue to work as his rig man and they would never talk about it again.

Rocky told Captain Aaron his version of the story. He also told him that when he fled Campeche after the killings, he headed to Cuba. He was arrested in Cuba and accused of being a gun runner. Fidel Castro hadn't been in power very long—five or six years. They threw him in prison. He spent eight years in the Cuban prison system. He told Captain Aaron that he almost died of starvation while in prison there. The meal portions were small. They were only fed twice a day—some kind of porridge in the mornings and beans in the afternoon. He ate roaches and any other kind of bugs he could get his hands on.

He was near death when the Cuban government decided to release him. He believed they set him free because they did not want an American to die in their prison. Rocky went on to tell Aaron he worked odd jobs in Florida for years until he decided to return to Port Isabel. He also told Captain Aaron that he was "okay" with the U.S. Government. In other words, he was "not a wanted man."

Captain Aaron told me (Rudy) that he believed Rocky *was* "okay" with the U.S. Government because he was a registered voter and had voted in several local elections.

Captain Aaron and Rocky never spoke about his past again. Rocky fished for Captain Aaron Moore on the *Trade Way* for five years. After that he retired from shrimping. He lived as a virtual recluse in a mobile home in Laguna Heights, Texas, for another twenty years or so. He kept to himself. He knew that the older people in town remembered his infamous past—he didn't want any problems. He just wanted to be left alone.

He got his wish. And that's how he died, a lone recluse—a broken old man who took his nightmarish memories to his grave.

Billy Holland was the first Texas shrimper to be caught fishing illegally in Mexican waters. After 1979 when Mexico stopped issuing fishing permits, Texas shrimpers continued going south during the fall.

Ironically, he wasn't caught fishing illegally by the Mexican Navy. It was the U.S. Coast Guard. Somehow, they found he had fished in Mexico and had Mexican fish and shrimp, so he was arrested and fined.

The Coast Guard used an old law passed in 1900 to make the bust. The Lacey Act prohibits and makes it illegal to trade, sell or transport shrimp, fish or other sea life caught illegally. They stated he was known to be fishing in Mexican waters illegally, he had fish and shrimp on board and he was transporting them.

Stories abound about the drinking and carousing when the boats anchored in Mexico. There are stories of men who had a family in Port Isabel and another one or more in some other port.

Once on the *Extreme*, Red Sagnes' boat, the header climbed up to the top of the rigging. When the captain asked what he was doing, he replied that he was watching TV. Realizing the guy had lost his sense of reality, he talked him down by promising to let him watch color TV below deck. Of course, this was in the days before color television existed. The guy agreed and they were able to get him below and lock the hatch to secure him until they reached shore.

Lanny Varnam remembers a particularly cold night of fishing in Mexican waters. He was with his brother,

Charles, and Ronald Boudreaux. Because they were in illegal waters, they risked being detected by the Mexican Navy gun boat. They had turned the lights off to drag the nets undetected. A cold norther blew in, making the night frigid. They came on a sandbar—and decided to drop anchor for the night to ride out the gusting wind. They were so close to shore they could hear the surf curling and crashing on the beach.

They spotted a small Mexican skiff a little further out from them.[1] The boat had no cabin and they could see the fishermen huddled around the small fire they had built on deck to provide some warmth. Lanny's crew watched as the fishermen blew hot breath air into their cupped hands before placing them over the fire for warmth. They felt sorry for them, as their small boat swayed back and forth and bounced up and down. The shivery sea sprayed them with ice cold Gulf water.

Lanny realized that these were fellow fishermen who were braving Mother Nature's rough weather. Even though they were in U.S. waters illegally, they too were fishing for survival. They were nautical miles away from safe harbor, families and no warm bed to sleep in.

He went to his bunk bed that wintry night thinking of the Mexican fishermen and the harsh, numbing conditions they worked under. He knew they came out of Bagdad Beach, east of Matamoros on the Mexican side. He hoped they would make it back to Bagdad safely. As the wind rattled riggings against the steel haul of their boat, the powerful north wind whistled in his

1 Mexican fisherman regularly fish U.S. waters for shark and snapper. They too run the risk of being caught and detained by the U.S. Coast Guard. If they are apprehended, the Coast Guard confiscates their boat, their motor, their nets and catch—and fines them.

ears. The ruffled, uneven swells rocked him to sleep. When he rose early the next morning, just as the sun light was breaking the eastern horizon, Lanny looked for the Mexican fishermen. He did not see them. They were gone.

One of the memories that sticks with Lanny to this day took place offshore from Rockport, Texas. They heard a distress call come over the radio that a shrimp boat was sinking. Any time a boat is in distress, and in a "mayday" situation, the captain or crew member who happens to be in charge makes the call over the radio. They give their longitude and latitude coordinates, as well as the cause of distress. Are they sinking? How fast are they taking on water? Are there mechanical problems? Does the boat have engine power? How many crew members? And injuries?

International maritime law requires that all marine vessels within reasonable proximity of the troubled vessel respond, react, aid and assist. They are required to let the distressed vessel know how far away they are, as well as let all other vessels in the area know of the distress call.

Fortunately, by the time they arrived on the scene, another boat had gotten there first and rescued the crew. The shrimp boat was deep in the water and sinking fast. Lanny found it both fascinating and depressing to watch the boat sink. It was one of those "slow motion" times as the stern sank into the water and the nose turned into the air. It started spinning and then everything turned quiet. They watched as the boat slowly disappeared into the water.

Lanny remembers another time during the late 1960s. They were out fishing when the weather report and Coast Guard issued a tempest storm warning. These kinds of warnings are quite common in the Gulf, especially during the summer and early fall months. A storm churned in the Gulf. The Coast Guard put out an all call for small marine vessels to seek safe harbor. One might assume that shrimp boats, sixty to seventy feet long, are big boats. The fact is they are not. They are smallish boats, by big boat standards. The Gulf of Mexico is a large body of water. During a tropical storms and hurricanes, the gale force winds can easily whip up huge billowing, surface waves reaching fifteen to twenty feet at their crest.

Climbing the violent face of a fifteen-to-twenty-foot storm swell and plummeting down off its back side is punishing. The relentless pounding of wave after wave for hours or even days will inflict tremendous damage on large marine vessels. It's easy to imagine the calamitous mutilation it will wreak to a sixty-to-seventy-foot shrimp boat.

The obvious common sense operating procedure for shrimp boat captains, when storm warnings are issued by the National Weather Service and the Coast Guard, is to seek safe harbor at the nearest port. Lanny and his good buddy, Billy Boynt, were ordered to remain on the boat in Port Aransas.

Every time a shrimp boat enters port for whatever the reason—repairs, refueling, or in this case safety from a storm—a crew member always stays behind on the boat, while the rest of the crew goes on shore. The crew member guards the boat's equipment and the typical thousands of pounds of shrimp loaded into the storage bins.

Unfortunately, the docks become a feeding ground for thieves, known to shrimpers as dock rats. These thieves know the minute a shrimp boat ties up at the dock. They don't care if the shrimp boat is a local boat belonging to a local company or if the boat belongs to another port. Everyone is fair game. They will steal and carry away any boat's cargo and goods. If a captain leaves his boat unguarded, especially overnight, after coming in to port, he is virtually inviting the thieves to freely help themselves to everything of value he and his crew have on the boat.

Every port has its bars. Most of them are located within close proximity to the docks. Ever since ancient mariner times, ports have accommodated seamen and their thirst for drink and fun. So when the rest of the crew went ashore to have a few beers and wait out a storm. Lanny and Billy stayed behind as guards.

They had secured the boat to the pilings and felt comfortable that the fastened lines were tight enough to ride out the storm. They watched as boat after boat came in, seeking safety from the approaching tempest. The boats that came in later began to tie up to the boat next to them. Thinking that the storm was not going to be that strong, the captains of the other boats apparently felt Lanny's boat would keep them moored safely. They didn't bother to run some of their lines to the dock pilings and tie themselves down. So many boats had docked in Port Aransas to ride out the storm that the harbor officials nearly closed off the channel. Hours later after the storm had passed, in the wee hours of the morning, the fishermen started making their way back to their boats. Some were "a little worse for the wear" after spending too much time in the bar.

A huge transport cargo ship had come up the channel. The powerful wake followed by the back suction of the big ship's draft began to pull the poorly tied boats loose. The tipsy fishermen suddenly heard several loud pops as they came closer to the dock. They soon realized what was happening. Their boat lines were popping. Boats were floating away! The befuddled crewmen shook the buzzed daze from their heads and began running towards the dislodged boats. The captains jumped behind their steering wheels, revved up their engines and began shouting orders.

A short while later all the scattered boats were rounded up and secured once again. Lanny's best memory was the repeated "pop, pop, pop," and the reactions and facial expressions of the fishermen. "If they'd only tied the boats up right," he laughed. Afterwards, when order was restored and all was calm, some of the captains and their crews popped open a few more. Lone Star and Pearl beer cans were emptied as the crews assessed the situation and joked about the incident. After all, they say that one of the best cures for a beer hangover is another ice cold beer. Lanny and Billy joined in.

Leif Varnam lived his horror story when he was a boy shrimping on his father's boat one summer. He was working on deck after they had picked up a trawl load. When the nets were emptied dropping their catch contents on deck, the ball-shaped mass of crammed sea life splattered. At this point, it's every creature for itself. Those that have legs like crabs scatter and scurry in all directions. Those that don't have legs, like Moray eels, slither like snakes on top of the sea-drenched deck also in every direction. They scramble for survival. A young kid of ten or twelve who is a first timer on a shrimp boat has no earthly idea what to expect as the nets are emptied of their contents.

At that life frightening moment, Leif was absolutely ly certain the giant monstrous eel had zeroed in on him. As a kid who had seen horror movies with giant grotesque man-eating creatures, Leif had no doubt it was his turn to be eaten alive. This was real life. It was not a horror movie. This gigantic slithering monster who was angry for being taken from its hiding place under the sea was coming after him and he panicked. Fear held him spell bound as the eel moved closer and closer. All of a sudden, with his heart throbbing at his throat, he jumped back and to one side, safely dodging the charging eel with its lance-sized teeth. Today he thinks back to that first time shrimping and laughs at his encounter with a moray eel. But back then Leif had no doubt in his mind that the eel wanted to make him its prey.

It wasn't uncommon for a shrimper to tell a story about seeing a UFO while sitting at the wheel alone during a dark night shift. Although most believe it's our government conducting some type of testing, others question that theory. According to Captain Noe Lopez, the night sky gets so black when you're out at sea, that sometimes crew members see things and objects that are not really there.

The rig man is the crew member who takes the second watch at the helm. The second watch usually starts after midnight and continues into the predawn. The rig man sits alone in the dark with his thoughts, drinking coffee and smoking cigarettes to help him stay awake and alert. There are full moon nights when the brilliant platinum face of the moon telescopes its silvery reflection on top of the rolling waves. As the escalating front side of an approaching wave is about to meet the prow of the boat, the moon's rippled reflection is visible. There are starlit nights with so many diamond twinkles blinking that a fisherman can feel the grace of God soothing his aloneness.

There are nights out at sea that are as black as India ink. A blackness so thick that it creates the spooky, uncomfortable feeling that frightening monsters lurk just beyond the onyx curtain. These are the times that a rig man gets out of the chair, serves himself another cup of coffee and lights up the next cigarette.

Some shrimpers have reported mysterious inexplicable lights appearing at a longitude position right in front of their eyes. The lights, round and bright in color, remain stationary as if observing them—moving slowly to the right, then back to center, then to the left. Then they dart away, disappearing beyond a human's eye distance of vision. They make no sound, at least no sound audible to the human ear.

Yes, the solitary thoughts of a shrimper alone at the night wheel of his boat during long lonely nights exercises his senses to extremes. He has to be experienced enough to realize what sightings are real, what sightings are high-flying airplanes traversing the Gulf, which are satellites or space shuttles looking down on us and which may be hallucinations. Optical illusions can be caused by fatigue, lack of sleep and an active imagination coupled with overactive senses.

Noe has seen balls of fire in the skies near Port Aransas and Louisiana. He and other captains have heard and sighted a possible submarine that appeared on the water's surface, about one-hundred feet from the boat.

He saw a shadow emerge out of the tall waves with curling whitecaps. The Poseidon-type figure had shimmering sea water cascading down its sides. Captain Noe put the boat's engine full throttle in reverse, tangling all the nets. This entanglement took him and his crew hours of hard labor to undo. It also cost them valuable lost hours of fishing time. He cannot explain many of the things he's seen nor does he want to. All he knows is that he has seen things that only shrimpers can see.

41

THE BLOCKADE,
THE VULCAN, THE PRIEST AND
THE BROOM PATROL

They fought to save their way of life

FATHER JOSEPH O'BRIEN, AN Oblate missionary and pastor of Our Lady Star of the Sea Catholic Church in Port Isabel, found himself knee-deep in a couple of political disputes involving the shrimping community. Having come from an assignment as a prison chaplain, he had faced adversity before. In fact, he was shot in the back during a prison riot. The prisoners had taken hostages. He negotiated with them to release the hostages and take him instead. After they agreed, something went awry and shots were fired.

He served six years as pastor of St. Joseph Parish in Brownsville and in 1987, came to Our Lady Star of the Sea Parish, where he remained until 2000. When he came to Port Isabel, he still carried the bullet in his back. Thankfully, his involvement in the town was less frightening. When he came to the Rio Grande Valley, he became involved with Valley Interfaith, which worked as a communal group to help people in need. It was here that Linda Sagnes, a local parishioner born in Port Isabel, got to know Father Joe. Linda was especially interested in issues having to do with shrimpers. Having grown up in the Mexiquito neighborhood of Port Isabel. Linda was familiar with shrimpers, their families and their way of life. Mexiquito is located along South Shore drive directly across the street from all the fish houses, shrimp boat docks and all the hustle and bustle of the industry. From early morning to late in the afternoon. Linda as well as all her neighbors lived with the constant sounds of gulls. As they took their early morning flight welcoming the golden sunrise, their squawking laughter called to everyone in the neighborhood to wake up and rise. A new day had arrived. The loud putt, putt cicada sound of the boat's bilge pumps filled the air. The putt, putting sound soon turned into a reverberating chorus of hubbub as the many shrimp boats moored along the water front joined in with their pumps. No one needed alarm clocks. These channel front sounds mixed with the wet smells of green sea weed left behind by the ebbing tide. These and other childhood memories and her strong Catholic faith aroused Linda's activism to join Father Joe O'Brien, shrimpers, their wives and others in their plight to save and preserve a robust way of life that had for so many years and generations made Port Isabel an economically vibrant, healthy community.

They worked on many social projects with churches of different denominations in the Rio Grande Valley that came together (under the umbrella of Valley Interfaith) focusing their efforts towards a better quality of life for the many rural poor colonia communities that existed and still exist today. They fought for better health care for children and families, better pre-school and early childhood educational services, street improvements and storm water drainage projects. These colonias for the most part were all developed with dirt roads. The land developers that plotted and subdivided the communities known as colonias wanted to maximize their profits. They bought cheap land out in rural parts of the county. Land that used to be farmland. Lax county building regulations allowed and permitted developers to subdivide and sell lots without enforcing any street drainage system.

These unpaved road conditions made it almost impossible for residents to get in or out of their community to work or anything else for that matter whenever a heavy rain fell. Every time they had a heavy downpour, standing rain water had nowhere to go. It became breeding grounds for disease carrying mosquitoes.

In 1988, a large boat loaded with hazardous chemicals, the *Vulcan*, sailed the Gulf of Mexico just a few miles off shore from Port Isabel and South Padre Island. The company wanted to burn its environmentally threatening chemicals in the Gulf. When the shrimpers asked for Father Joe's help, without hesitation, he immediately joined the fight to stop the burning. "They would destroy something they know nothing about," he told the press.

Later, the National Marine Fisheries for some misguided reason wanted to ban commercial fishing in the U.S. waters of the Gulf of Mexico. Texas shrimpers, in an act of defiance and protest to a government's decision to put an end to their livelihood, once again banded together. They decided to block the jetty entries at Port Aransas and the Port of Brownsville with their shrimp boats, not allowing any marine vessels to enter or exit the two ports. Father Joe discouraged the blockade telling the shrimpers to seek other means of negotiating with U.S. fishery officials. He felt that the blockade would impede marine vessels in need of assistance from reaching safe harbor. However, the shrimpers moved forward. In Aransas, approximately one hundred boats blocked the jetty pass. Because the distance between the jetties at Brazos de Santiago Pass in Port Isabel is narrow, it only took about twenty boats to block entry. The Port Isabel Coast Guard station officials ignored the blockade, but the Corpus Coast Guard issued citations to shrimp boat captains in Aransas.

Father Joe joined in the fight to save the industry, and eventually was designated by the shrimpers to take the lead voice in their fight against the government. They traveled to New Orleans to attend public hearings being held by U.S. Congressmen and Senators that sat on the U.S. fishery committees. The law makers were there mostly to hear what and why U.S. fishery officials wanted to shut down commercial fishing for U.S. shrimpers.

The hearing was initially set up as a mere formality. The Congressman were going to listen to both sides, but they were leaning towards the recommendations presented by U.S. Fisheries representatives and their skewed studies. The studies presented by the government office blamed the shrimpers for the declining population of the Kemp Ridley sea turtle as well as the red snapper population.

According to U.S. Fisheries, the trawling method used by U.S. shrimpers caused the decline and they needed to be stopped.

Father Joe and busloads of local shrimpers, their wives and supporters traveled to New Orleans. They were just as determined to save their jobs and livelihood as the National Fisheries officials were in shutting them down.

Before the meeting Father Joe met with the group of shrimper families. He told the women to bring their brooms. The shrimper wives didn't know why Father Joe wanted them to bring them and in fact they thought his request was funny. But they knew he had a reason and they trusted him. He called them the "Broom Patrol." He banned guns, saying that brooms would do the trick. When they arrived in New Orleans, Father Joe and an Exxon executive engaged in a loud argument. The louder the discussion became, the more Linda Sagnes worried. Finally, she yelled "Broom Patrol!" Twelve women with brooms surrounded Father Joe, six on each side. The argument ended.

The meeting with the Congressmen and Marine Fisheries officials was held as scheduled. Although the meeting room was small, the shrimpers were not going to be denied attendance. They crammed in and stood arms crossed, shoulder-to-shoulder, lined up against the perimeter of the crowded room. Marine Fisheries officials did not anticipate the room full of angry, serious shrimpers staring at them. They were familiar with the boat blockade that had occurred before and realized that the shrimpers would not go down without a fight. They understood that lawmakers were not going to approve their commercial fishing ban recommendations.

The Congressmen who were present got the picture too. By the time the meeting ended, the National Marine Fisheries dropped the ban proposal.

They did not realize nor expect that they going up against a tenacious, old feisty Irish priest who had placed himself in harm's way many times before for causes that were important to him and his parishioners. Besides, he had God on his side.

NOE LOPEZ'S VERSION OF THE BLOCKADE:

In 1989, Captain Noe Lopez, was working for Bill Zimmerman, a local shrimp boat fleet owner when the shrimpers blockaded the Brownsville Ship Channel (rather than the jetties) to protest the TED regulation. The blockade consisted of ninety-seven boats tied together with ⅜" chain links. All of the boats were steel-hulled. None of the Port Isabel boats carried guns, but some boats from other regions did. The Port Isabel/South Padre Island Coast Guard threatened to break up the blockade, but in the end they did little to stop them.

A casino gaming boat that was doing business out of the Port Isabel Navigation District left the bay with a boat filled with gambling passengers for its cruise. The shrimpers told the captain he was not going to be allowed to sail his ship back past them. The captain ignored the warning and when he returned, he didn't stop for the blockade. He defiantly plowed into the first line of boats. Breaking through the first line of defense, the captain kept going. As he approached the second line of shrimp boats chained together, shots were fired from the angry shrimpers. Realizing that the shrimpers were serious and fearing for the safety of his crew and passengers, the casino captain put his boat in reverse and returned back into the open waters of the Gulf of Mexico and safety.

The shrimpers felt that their governor and senator played them wrong. They had promised to remove the TED requirements. After the fourth day of blockading any maritime ships and vessels from entering or exiting the Brazos de Santiago Pass and Brownsville ship channel, the shrimpers were convinced to break up the blockade.

UPI NEWS ARCHIVES: JULY 23, 1989:

Some shrimpers continued to block the Brownsville Ship Channel near Port Isabel at middday, the Coast Guard said. But 85 to 90 shrimpers continued Sunday night to block the Brownsville Ship Channel near Port Isabel.

'Basically, they say they're going to stay there until the whole issue on TEDs is resolved, is the statement they've been making to us,' said Petty Officer Clifton Vigus.

'We have accomplished what we set out to do,' Mialjevich told UPI. 'I think the public now realizes how this has been a frame-up of the shrimping industry. What we have done is put Secretary Mosbacher back at the bargaining table with our congressmen.'

Mialjevich said shrimpers want Mosbacher to postpone laws requiring fishermen to use the devices, known as TEDs, until a study by the National Academy of Sciences determines the effect on sea turtles of shrimping operations and whether TEDs can cut their mortality rate.

Turtle Excluder Device (TED)

42

ENVIRONMENTAL REGULATIONS

> We balance out nature.
>
> Charles Burnell

AS THE DEMAND FOR shrimp grew, fishermen continued to build bigger and better boats. Nearly 800 boats called the Rio Grande Valley home in the industry's heyday.

As the boat population increased and the sea turtle population decreased over the years, many environmentalists blamed the shrimping industry. They argued that the turtles got caught up in the nets and died.

The TED (turtle excluder device) is the direct result of legislation to protect them. Although most of the shrimpers we interviewed felt that catching turtles had never been a problem, they abided by the rules they disliked.

The first TED devices frustrated the shrimpers tremendously. The devices were cumbersome to handle at first. They were not used to them and the safety issue came into play because of this. Being the resourceful people that they are they soon adapted. They had to, they had no choice. The significant loss of shrimp caused by the TED bothered the shrimpers. Shrimp came into the nets, but some of them were also extracted. The loss of shrimp translated into a loss of revenue, and that was not a good thing for shrimpers. In fact, the reduction in the amount of shrimp caught, compounded with the rising cost of fuel and other increasing operating costs, created an additional financial burden for shrimpers. Something they did not need during a time when so many of them were struggling to keep up with bank debts.

They were no longer thinking of making a profit. At the minimum, all they wanted was to break even for the year. So that perhaps they could survive to be able to fish the following year. The percentage of shrimp that was lost at first was not known. Government studies estimated that 3% - 13% of the shrimp catch would be lost to TEDS. Many shrimpers reported that they were losing more than the 13% estimated by the scientific studies funded by the government. They were reporting up to 20% loss. These reports were countered by researchers saying that as shrimpers adapted and learned to use the TED as intended, the percentage of shrimp that were escaping would decrease.

Shrimpers became alarmed at the high numbers of shrimp they were losing. So in order to keep their industry sustainable, they decided through their shrimping associations to take action on their own behalf. They contacted field operations individuals that had been involved or were interested in developing better methods, as well as improve TEDS. They wanted to help and be contributors to saving the turtles. They had already been blamed by the different environmental groups and the government for endangering the survival of the species.

The last thing they wanted was to be identified as the industry that caused the extinction of the Kemp's Ridley turtle. But just as important, they could not afford to become an extinct industry. There was too much at stake. Shrimping was all they knew how to do. They had to do something, and they did. They needed to find a solution. They needed a win, win outcome.

Charles Burnell credits Gary Graham, a marine fisheries specialist from Sea Grant Texas, with adapting the TED into an acceptable and workable device with the least amount of shrimp loss. It took a few years and a lot of trial and error to improve the device. Unfortunately, many of the independent boat owners did not have the financial resources to weather the change. They either sold their boats to big companies or the banks took the boats.

The last thing the bank wanted was to take a shrimp boat for non-payment of a loan. They were in the business of lending money and getting their money back with a return profit in interest. They knew nothing about operating a shrimp boat. Suddenly some local banks had become boat owners. The boats they owned were tied to the dock and listed as a liability on their books. They had lost lots of money with them, and now they were still losing money.

The boats sat idle, deteriorating. The situation became so bad that banks asked shrimpers to take the boats. They were willing to hand the boats over to individuals willing to take them. All the banks asked in return was that those persons who agreed to work the boat, pay down on the loan balance. There were not many takers. It takes thousands and thousands of dollars to prep a boat to go out on a fishing trip. Most people did not have the money. The ones who did knew the bankrupt boats were in bad shape.

They had been left inoperable tied to the dock for too long. It was going to take huge amounts of money to fix them back up to fishing condition. So the boats just sat there rusting away.

The National Marine Fisheries designed the first TED. Shrimpers adapted it to lose the fewest shrimp possible and the owners began installing them in their nets. Many make their own TEDs today. Later, a requirement for a fish excluder device became law. This too was another blow to their profits. Shrimpers were now being held responsible to catch and release the by-catch that entered the nets. They were blamed for the decline of the red snapper population.

Never mind the thousands of game and sports fishermen who went after the snapper every day they could. Never mind all of the oil rig workers who spent hours of their off time fishing for snapper. Never mind all of the offshore supply crew boat workers who fished for red snapper while they waited for their next assignment. They were not factored into the problem of the red snapper decline. Only the shrimpers were.

Most shrimpers still feel, believe and say, they were not responsible for the decline of sea turtles because the turtles mainly float near the surface and they drag the bottom. Their main objection was due to the ten-to-fifteen percent or more loss of their shrimp catch.

Robert Vela started shrimping with his dad when he was a teenager back in the 1960s. During all the time he went shrimping he doesn't remember ever catching a turtle in his nets. "I sometimes saw them on the top of the water. Our nets dragged the bottom. Turtles are smart. They can avoid the nets."

Billy Holland also noted that the turtles swim on top of the water, not at the bottom. He felt that TEDs don't work. With the added requirement of a fish excluder, he estimated at least a ten-percent drop in shrimp.

In a lifetime of fishing, Charles Burnell only netted three, maybe four, turtles. He recalled catching a big shark one time, cutting it open and finding a turtle inside. He couldn't believe the turtle didn't have a mark on him. "That shark must have swallowed it whole," he said.

Charles's pet peeve is that bycatch regulations prevent boats from bringing in fish caught in the nets. The fish are caught incidentally and are not the catch shrimpers are after. By the time the nets are brought up on deck and emptied, the fish are almost dead. The headers job is to begin heading shrimp as soon as the catch is spread out on deck, the nets out of the way and back in the water. The rig man too has his job to do. He has to ready the nets and return them back to the water. The captain needs to be at the wheel steering and keeping clear of any danger ahead, to his sides and in back of him. There are always other boats in the area and the wheel cannot be left unattended.

Stopping to collect the bycatch that is not allowed to be brought back by the shrimpers, to throw it overboard, takes too much time away from their job responsibilities. Shrimp are not resilient. They spoil and turn bad fast. They need to be headed, washed and iced down (refrigerated/frozen) right away.

After all the shrimp are headed and stored away, the header needs to clear the deck clean of all debris (shrimp heads and all other by catch) for the next nets to be brought up on deck. So by the time the bycatch are thrown back to the sea they are dead. The only things that benefit from the trash thrown overboard are the sharks that trail along the sides of the boat. They swallow everything whole. The shrimpers argue that since the fish are already dead, why not let the crew keep them. Headers especially could benefit from taking fish home to feed their families.

Mike Zimmerman lamented the many state and federal commercial fishing regulations. They have brought a great financial burden to shrimpers. The cost of operating a shrimp boat keeps going up with the introduction and implementation of every new regulation. It appears to shrimpers that the continuous creation of new laws are specifically directed towards shrimpers and their fishing methods. The emotional sentiment among shrimpers is that the environmentalist, with the government on their side, are trying to put them out of business. "It costs more than $200 for each TED." He feels that recreational fishing and oil spills had more negative impact on turtles.

Although there are programs to help farmers and agricultural workers, no similar programs exist for shrimpers and fishermen. Linda Sagnes pointed out that the SBA did loan them money to buy a boat.

Appendix

A1

Shrimpers Working Together

Southern Shrimp Alliance
Tarpon Springs, FL
John Williams, Executive Director

The Southern Shrimp Alliance (SSA) represents the shrimping industry in eight states: Alabama, Florida, Georgia, Louisiana, Mississippi, North Carolina, South Carolina and Texas.

∽

Texas Shrimp Association
Brownsville, TX
Andrea Hance, Executive Director

The Texas Shrimp Association (TSA) is a non-profit organization dedicated to providing strategies and educating consumers, lawmakers, press, environmental groups, and the public about the importance of wild-caught Texas Gulf Shrimp.

∽

Texas Sea Grant

Texas Sea Grant is a unique partnership that unites the resources of the federal government, the State of Texas and universities across the state to create knowledge, tools, products and services that benefit the economy, the environment, and the citizens of Texas.

∽

Gary Graham, retired Marine Fisheries Extension Specialist, worked extensively with Texas shrimpers in the adoption of the TEDs, BRDs (Bycatch Reduction Devices) and fuel-efficient steel trawl doors. One of Charles Burnell's boat was the first in the Port Isabel/Brownsville market to test the trawl gear.

In an article in Texas Shores, Andrea Hance, Executive Director of the Texas Shrimp Association, said:

"He has made a tremendous, positive impact on our industry in every facet... With each set of industry challenges, Gary led a team that researched, developed and implemented gear modifications, specifically by catch reduction, trawl net exclusion, and cataloging of bottom obstructions, just to name a few. Through his hard work and dedication, the commercial shrimping industry is now considered to be one of the most sustainable fisheries in the world."

Tony Reisinger, Coastal and Marine Resources Agent for Cameron County, works with the Brownsville//Port Isabel shrimp fleet. He has developed strong working relationships with the shrimpers.

RUDY H. GARCIA

Rudy H. Garcia resides with his wife Rita in Laguna Vista, Texas. They are blessed with four lovely daughters—Risa, Mari, Marisa, and Carisa. They also have four beautiful grandchildren—Gia, Iris, Maya, and Alejandra.

Rudy shares his love of poetry in his first published book, *Life Renewed*, where he expresses romance from the beginning and his love for family and his faith which is everlasting. Born and raised in the Laguna Madre community, Rudy spent much of his childhood exploring the shores of the Laguna Madre, walking the length of the shrimp docks, venturing in and out of shrimp houses, boarding shrimp boats and conversing with the crew. When he was old enough to work on board a shrimp boat, his father sent him to experience the sea with his Uncle Joe and his Cousin Eddie.

Living in this area, it was customary to shop the Matamoros market frequently and explore some of Mexico's most beautiful cities. In 1983, after being married for six years, Rudy and his wife Rita traveled as a couple to Mexico City to visit the shrine of our blessed Virgen de Guadalupe, where they made their petition—and nine months later they were blessed with their first daughter. So that spiritual bond and faith with God and our Blessed Mother has been truly instrumental in their family's daily lives.

PAT MCGRATH AVERY

Pat McGrath Avery first visited Port Isabel in 1974 when she brought her parents to spend the winter. The number of shrimp boats amazed and thrilled her. It also aroused her curiosity.

During that visit, she told her family that someday she wanted to live there. Fast-forward twenty years to after her children were grown, when she and her husband moved to the Valley. Everything had changed in the shrimping industry, but nothing had changed in her interest.

She met Rudy Garcia at one of his poetry readings where he told stories about his youth and shrimping adventures. A mutual friend, Sally Scaman, suggested that they write the history of the shrimping years in Port Isabel.

A few months later in early 2018, they began interviewing the men who lived and worked on shrimp boats and in shrimp-related businesses. They researched and read all the material they could find about the glory years, when shrimping put Port Isabel and Brownsville on the world map.

Pat loves to research and write nonfiction books that teach her and her readers about unknown pieces of our history. Together with Rudy, she takes pride in telling the stories of the men and women who lived and worked as a community to improve their livelihoods and their town.

Index

C

D

CPSIA information can be obtained
at www.ICGtesting.com
Printed in the USA
LVHW080743080120
642888LV00007B/81/P

9 781943 267736